PERCEPTION AND PHOTOGRAPHY

Richard D. Zakia

ROCHESTER INSTITUTE OF TECHNOLOGY, ROCHESTER, N.Y.

LIGHT IMPRESSIONS CORPORATION, Rochester, New York

Library of Congress Cataloging in Publication Data

Zakia, Richard D.
  Perception and photography

    1. Composition (Photography). 2. Visual perception.
3. Gestalt psychology. I. Title
TR179.Z34   770'.11   74-3402
ISBN 0-87992-015-7
(Previously ISBN 0-13-656934-X)

To Lois and Renee

10   9   8   7   6   5   4   3   2

*Printed in the United States of America
Cover design by Constance Shermer*

*Also by Richard D. Zakia.
Perceptual Quotes for Photographers, 1980
Visual Concepts for Photographers, 1980*
Available through Light Impressions.
For free catalog write:
  Light Impressions Corporation
  P.O. Box 3012
  Rochester, NY 14614

Light Impressions Corporation, Rochester, New York

Contents

Foreword   9

Preface   11

1. Introduction   13

2. Ganzfeld   18

3. Figure-Ground   20

4. Gestalt Laws   32

5. Prägnanz   79

6. Summary   85

7. Gestalt Exercises   112

8. Gestalt Games   136

   Appendix   151

   References   154

   Index   162

Foreword

I first knew Professor Zakia years ago as one of my students at the Rochester Institute of Technology. Upon graduation he took a position with Eastman Kodak Co. as a photographic engineer. His interest in education and students led him to become a teacher of photographic science at RIT, famed for teachers who actually care for their students. His forte was leading young people to see that science can be beautiful. While teaching he was expanding his interest and experience to include education as a whole, receiving his doctorate in educational psychology from the University of Rochester in 1969. He is currently Coordinator of the MFA Program in Photography at RIT.

A wedding between Gestalt psychology and photography is long overdue, and it will still be a while before it fully happens. However, Professor Richard D. Zakia has at least introduced the two arts to each other in terms that make their natural affinity unmistakable. Should this book get the attention it merits, the wedding will be inevitable. Other thinkers and writers will build on his firm foundation and eventually join the two fields together as one.

Photography and Gestalt psychology could be indentical twins or two sides of a one-sided coin, yet they have long been separated by a seemingly insurmountable difference in vocabularies. In photography alone, the specialized jargon problem is so serious that most photographers and photographic scientists never master it. This is likewise true of Gestalt psychology. Thus it takes a person with a considerable gift for language to bridge the chasm between them. Professor Zakia has done this in his own mind, then found a way to translate his understanding into a basic text that can be understood by photographers.

Though all photographers should study Gestalt psychology, and vice versa, it is not likely that this would come about accidentally. Furthermore, there are numerous obstacles preventing it, not just the jargon barrier. The overall problem is reciprocal ignorance, neither photographer nor psychologist having more than a hazy notion of what the other one is up to. Perhaps this is basically the fear of confusion, with each being afraid of getting lost in the other's field of knowledge. Another problem is pride: Neither photographer nor psychologist would deign to bow to the other's understanding.

The barriers are many, but they can all be bridged. However, only a loving man can do it, for knowledge without love is a treadmill. Such a man we have in Richard D. Zakia. His splendid little book is the humble foundation on which the bridge can be built. And it *will* be built if you give Zakia's thought and sensitivity the respect that they deserve.

Ralph Hattersley

Preface

"By reviewing the old we learn the new" goes an old Chinese proverb. By reviewing the Gestalt laws of visual perception, which were formulated in the early 1900's, I have gained new insights into visual design and composition.

Perception and Photography is a modest attempt to select a few of the Gestalt laws and to present them in a highly visualized manner. I believe the laws I have chosen are basic, easily grasped, highly relevant, and generalizable to all areas of visual design.

I have used photographs, paintings, graphic designs, and type designs to illustrate the Gestalt laws. This not only reinforces visually what is said verbally but also demonstrates the variety of disciplines in which the laws apply. I could just as easily have illustrated the Gestalt laws using television, fabrics, magazine layouts, floral designs, interior designs, cosmetology, clothing design, etc. This book, therefore, although addressed to photographers and graphic designers, is really intended for anyone seriously concerned in the shaping or making of visual messages and visual environments. We all have a common purpose—visual communication and expression.

In the last section of the book you will find some Gestalt exercises and games. The intent is to provide further reinforcement of the Gestalt laws and, perhaps, even a little fun.

I am grateful to the many persons who have helped me in the preparation of this book—particularly to my wife, Lois; my students over the years; my secretary, Bernie Jordan; and to Roger Remington, Hollis Todd, Larry McKnight, and Mark Wollwage. My thanks also to all those who have kindly allowed me to use their photographs and illustrations.

Richard D. Zakia
Rochester, N.Y.

This recognition, in real life, of a rhythm of surfaces, lines, and values is for me the essence of photography; composition should be a constant of preoccupation, being a simultaneous coalition— an organic coordination of visual elements.

—*HENRI CARTIER BRESSON*

Ideally I want every piece analyzed, technically, structurally, formally. And I want it to come out shatteringly integrated, like a crystal, totally whole, defying analysis.

—*MICHAEL TILSON*
Music Director and Conductor

To design is to plan and to organize, to order, to relate and to control.

—*JOSEF ALBERS*

1. Introduction

It may, at first, seem peculiar to begin a book on photography by talking about psychology. But it seems less peculiar when you consider that the practice and understanding of photography are concerned with chemistry, physics, optics, mathematics, and engineering; that the taking and experiencing of photographs are concerned with art, design, and psychology. A photographer can learn much about making pictures by studying art, design, and such branches of psychology as perception, motivation, learning theory, and personality theory.

In this book I will stress how knowledge of one area of psychology—visual perception—can help a photographer make better photographs. The rationale for this approach is very simple. A photographer makes pictures. People look at pictures. If the photographer knows something about the process of looking or seeing, he can then design pictures that facilitate seeing, that help the viewer to see what he intends to communicate through his pictures. Visual perception is a study of the process of seeing. But visual perception does not involve the eye and sight alone. Certainly the eyes are necessary for seeing, just as are the ears for hearing, the nose for smelling, the tongue for tasting, and the skin for feeling. However, it is important to keep in mind that *visual perception involves all the senses and, also, the memory.* What we experience as seeing is interconnected with many other things. I am reminded of the old spiritual that tells of how all "them bones" are connected; the head bone to the neck bone, the neck bone to the shoulder bone, and so forth. When we think of perception we can think of it as a process in which all "them senses" and that which we call memory are connected.

**Visual
Elements**

Throughout this book the term visual element will be used to refer, in a general way, to any kind of a visual stimulus that is readily seen as a discrete unit. For example, a visual element can be a letter in an alphabet. In the English alphabet there are twenty-six such visual elements. Each one is a discrete unit having a recognizable and familiar shape.

The letter Z, for example, can be referred to as a single visual element. It need not be made up of a single visual element such as one continuous area, however. It can be made up of two, three, four, or five visual elements.

Regardless of the number of discrete visual elements, we can still perceive these elements in such a way that they are automatically *grouped* and seen as the familiar letter Z. This is because each visual element is in close proximity to every other and is oriented in such a way as to make it easy to see the *whole* letter Z and not the individual *parts.*

A visual element need not be a letter. It is anything we see as a recognizable, discrete unit. It can be a paper clip, rubber band, pencil, coin, circle, square, etc.

*Visual elements
can vary in* size
Z Z Z z

*Visual elements
can vary in* shape
Z Z Z Z z

*Visual elements
can vary in* color
(hue, chroma, value)
Z Z Z

*Visual elements
can vary in* texture
Z Z

Visual elements can also vary in mass, time, and so on. They can be similar (▲ ◆ ▼) or dissimilar (● ▲ ✚).

The purpose of this book is to set forth a few basic principles to assist a photographer (or anyone else involved in the design and production of visual images) to gain new insights into how visual elements can be arranged to facilitate perception—to facilitate grouping.

**Gestalt
Psychology**

The study of visual perception is very broad. It includes many concepts such as detection, discrimination, resolution, manipulation, attention, selection, channel capacity, interference, illusion, storage and retrieval, etc. This book concerns itself with one aspect of visual perception—how man organizes information, something psychologists have known for many years through experimentation, and philosophers and artists through intuition. The Gestalt school of psychology, which was originated in Germany about 1912 by Dr. Max Wertheimer, provides us with some simple and convincing evidence about how man organizes and groups visual elements so that they are perceived as wholes. In other words, what you experience when you look at a photograph is quite different from what you would experience were you to look at each item in the photograph separately.

Gestalt

The whole is different from the sum of its parts. In Fig. 1 a person can choose to see each visual element (the individual letters) separately or as grouped to form the shape of a camera.

Seeing the camera is seeing the totality of the visual elements. This grouping of visual elements into a single figure is Gestalt. (Further examples are shown in Figs. 2 and 3.)

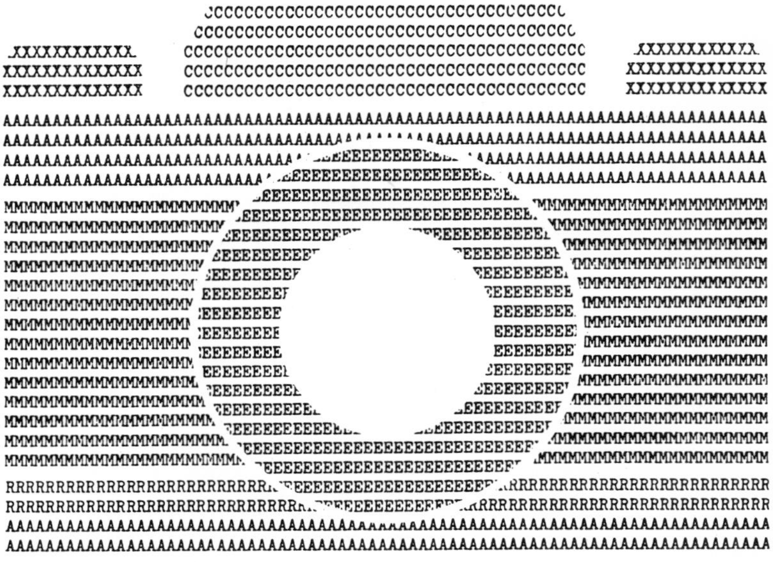

Figure 1.

An example of Gestalt; the camera as a whole is different from the sum of the visual elements.

TRIUMPH
DES JAHRES

by Johann M. Voltz

*(Courtesy
John Hay Library,
Brown University)*

Figure 2.

*The hat represents the Prussian eagle digging its claws into Napoleon.
The visual elements that make up the face are the countless dead caused by
Napoleon's lust for fame and power.*

CAMOUFLAGE SUIT
FOR OCT. 1966

by R. F. Heinecken

Figure 3. Photographic montage.

2. Ganzfeld

Imagine for a moment a visual world in which there are no visual elements. You are able to see but what is in your visual field is completely homogeneous. The situation I am trying to describe does not exist in our heterogeneous visual world. But you can imagine, for example, looking into a large integrating sphere or being at an altitude of 10,000 feet where all that can be seen is an overcast sky. You can also imagine yourself standing in front of an 18% graycard that is one mile square. Such imaginary situations approximate a homogeneous visual field or *Ganzfeld.* What kind of a visual experience does a Ganzfeld provide? You can find out for yourself by closing one eye and covering the other with a diffusing shell such as a white plastic spoon. Look at a uniform source of light through a saturated green filter. After a few minutes the saturated green color is seen as a neutral gray. The same phenomenon occurs with other colors.

When a visual field is completely homogeneous we are unable to make discriminations. Place any object (for example, a pencil) in the Ganzfeld and the color will begin to reappear. For visual discrimination to take place the visual world must be heterogeneous. A person sees by making comparisons—by discrimination.

Figure 4.

Homogeneous and heterogeneous fields.

HOMOGENEOUS VISUAL FIELD (GANZFELD)

HETEROGENEOUS VISUAL FIELD

Figure-Ground   The black triangle in the white square represents a simple heterogeneous visual field (Fig. 4). The triangle, like all visual shapes and forms, possesses at least two distinguishable aspects called *figure* and *ground.* Several important observations can be made regarding figure-ground relationships:

1. Even though the figure and ground are in the same physical plane, the figure often appears nearer to the observer.
2. Figure and ground cannot be seen simultaneously, but can be seen sequentially. (With a little effort you can see a white square with a triangular hole.)
3. Figure usually occupies an area smaller than does ground.
4. Figure is seen as having contour; ground is not.
5. Figure is seen as having shape or form quality; ground is not (except of course when ground is seen as figure, as in the case of a white square with a triangular hole).

In the heterogeneous world in which we live a person is free to select what he considers figure. In a given situation different people will see different things as figure, depending on a variety of circumstances. For example, different people walking down a main street will, at any instant and depending on their interests, see:

a) a clock telling the time of day if they are hurrying to a meeting;
b) a theatre if they are looking for entertainment;
c) a bus or taxi if they are looking for transportation (Fig. 5).

Figure-ground relationships are used in many diagnostic tests. Most of us have taken tests for color blindness in which we try to group certain color spots to see a number. The inability to discriminate among colors and to group some as figure identifies the presence of color blindness.

CLOCK   THEATRE   TAXI

Figure 5. Figure-ground is a selective process.

3. Figure-Ground

Whenever we look at something, that which we see as an object is called *figure* and is always seen against some background. The first step in perception is distinguishing figure from ground. Sometimes it is easy to see figure against ground. Sometimes it is not. What factors contribute to our perception of figure? Why do we see things as we do? A powerful and convincing demonstration of figure-ground was presented by K. Koffa in 1922. He used an equivocal fence phenomenon (Fig. 6). Look at it and describe what you see. Your first impression might well be that of black lines against a white background area. If so, the black lines are figure. A simple concept, isn't it? But let's continue. Look at it a little longer and you might see four narrow white stripes, bars, or fence slats. If you do, the white areas of strips are figure and the remainder of the picture is ground. But why do you see the four narrow stripes as figures? A simple answer is that it is easier to see the narrow stripes, but it explains nothing. A better answer is that the two lines that make up the narrow slat are closer together and, therefore, there is a greater tendency for the viewer to group them into some figure. Three important points can be made here:

1. One can predict that the closer together two elements are, the greater the probability that they will be grouped together and seen as figure. (This is called the law of proximity and will be discussed in more detail later.)
2. It is impossible to have figure without ground. Put differently, what we call background in a picture is very important.
3. It is nearly impossible to see the four narrow slats and the three wide slats simultaneously. You cannot have figure without ground.

The figure-ground relationship in Fig. 6 can be enhanced by taking a pencil and darkening the narrow stripes.

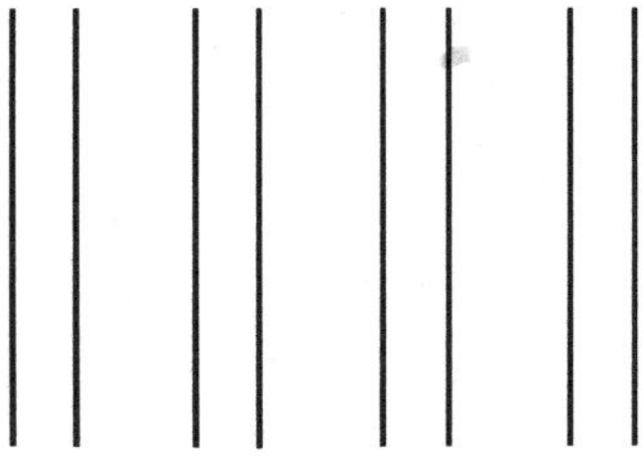

Figure 6.

Equivocal fence phenomenon. What do you see?

**Figure-Ground
Boundary**

Fig. 7 shows a single contour line that serves as a boundary for the facial profile of an old man and the head and torso profile of a woman. It is possible to see either the woman or the man. When the old man is seen it is because the opposite side of the contour line has become ground. The converse, of course, occurs when you see the woman. (On page 72 you will see how closure can facilitate your seeing either figure.)

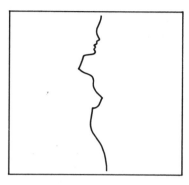

Figure 7.

*Figure-ground boundary.
Profile of an old man or head
and torso profile of a woman?*

**Graphic
Symbols**

The concept of figure-ground is used extensively by artists in the design of graphic symbols. Fig. 8 is an example of an effective use of figure-ground (positive-negative space).

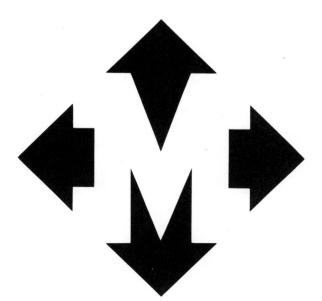

Figure 8.

*Figure-ground. If you decide
that the dark areas are figure,
you see arrows. If you decide
that the light areas contained
within the dark area are figure,
you see a letter. (Courtesy
Mapco Inc., Tulsa, Oklahoma)*

Photographs   Photographs can be described in terms of figure-ground. Some
provide interesting abstract patterns that are greatly enhanced
when color and texture are present (Fig. 9).

GEYSER OVERFLOW   by Jerry Hagner

Figure 9. Figure-ground photograph.

What's in a Name?

The term figure-ground may be new to some photographers and artists, but the concept is not. Artists and photographers often refer to it as *positive-negative space.* Different disciplines seem to have different vocabularies for describing the same concept. Such exclusiveness in terminology is further demonstrated in the field of communications engineering where the term *signal-to-noise ratio* is used to quantitatively describe figure-ground. All three areas of endeavor are, unfortunately, using different word labels to describe a similar concept. Recognizing that we may be using different words to describe the same concept can improve communications among the various disciplines.

Discipline	Label
Psychology	Figure-ground
Art and photography	Positive-negative space
Engineering	Signal/noise ratio

Figs. 10, 11, 12, 13, 14, and 15 show examples of figure-ground, positive-negative space, and signal/noise ratio from the point of view of a psychologist, artist and designer, photographer, and photographic and television engineer.

When the figure-ground or negative-positive space are similar or when the signal/noise ratio is low, perception is usually very difficult. Conversely when the signal/noise ratio is high, we have a good figure-ground relationship. Perception and, therefore, communications, are improved. For example, in Fig. 6 we could make it easier for a person to see the narrow stripes as figure by darkening them. By doing this we have increased contrast (as a photographer might say) or increased the signal/noise ratio (as a photographic engineer might say). In any case, a better figure-ground relationship is established. (Does darkening the wider stripes change your perception of figure-ground? Try it. Make a few copies of Fig. 6, darken them differently and test them out with your friends.)

EXAMPLES OF
FIGURE-GROUND
RELATIONSHIPS
FOR DIFFERENT
DISCIPLINES.

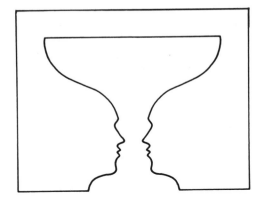

Figure 10.

*Figure-ground
(psychologist).
Goblet or profiles?
Such a figure-ground
reversal was first
shown by the
Danish psychologist,
Edgar Rubin, in 1915.*

Figure 11.

*Figure-ground—
positive-negative
space (artist).*

SKY AND WATER I,
1938

by Escher

Design by
Steve Chapman
and Tom Morin

Figure 12.

*Figure-ground—
positive-negative
space (designer).*

by Roger Remington

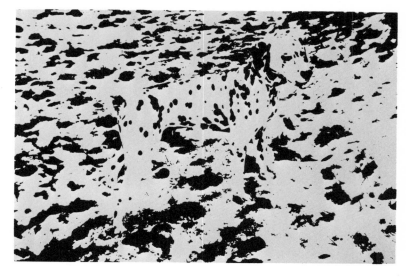

Figure 13.

Figure-ground—positive-negative space (photographer). Some spots are selected from the complete field of spots and, because of their relationship, are grouped to form the shape of a dog. (See Appendix, p. 151.)

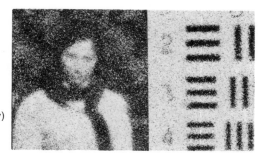

PHOTOGRAPH (grainy)

by Carl Franz

Figure 14.

Figure-ground— signal/noise ratio (photographic engineer).

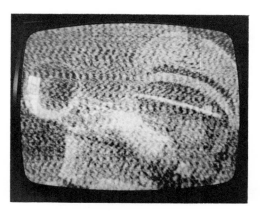

Figure 15.

Figure-ground— signal/noise ratio (television engineer).

**Graininess
and Noise**

Photographic engineers, in designing photographic systems, use the same terminology as other engineers in communications. For example, part of the noise in a photographic system of visual communication is granularity or graininess. A photograph that is very grainy contains a high level of visual noise which causes the picture (visual information) to be difficult to see. The information (signal) contained in the picture lacks clarity because of the large amount of grain (noise). The picture, therefore, has a low signal to noise ratio. Photographers can increase the signal/noise ratio by reducing the level of graininess. They do so by selecting a fine-grain film, a fine-grain developer, a larger format film so that high magnification from negative to print is not required, etc.

Resolving power targets are often used in photography to determine how well a photographic system can reproduce repetitive lines that decrease in width and space (spatial frequency). If you consider the number of black bars you can distinguish as signal, you readily see how graininess adds to the noise level and makes the visual signal less distinguishable (Fig. 16). A similar situation exists when slides are projected on a screen; the picture takes on the texture of the screen (Fig. 17).

by Carl Franz

Figure 16.

*Resolving power targets as figure-ground.
Increasing amounts of graininess
lower the signal/noise ratio, causing
a poor figure-ground relationship.*

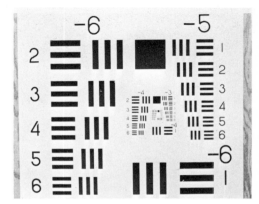

GOOD FIGURE-GROUND (HIGH SIGNAL/NOISE)

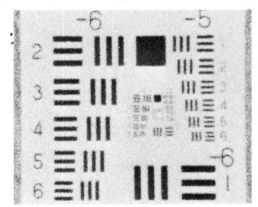

FAIR FIGURE-GROUND (MODERATE SIGNAL/NOISE)

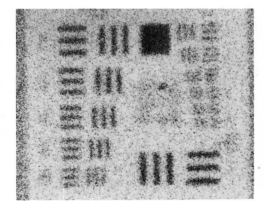

POOR FIGURE-GROUND (LOW SIGNAL/NOISE)

 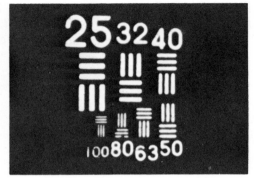

LENTICULAR SCREEN

Figure 17. The figure-ground quality of projected slides is dependent upon the surface characteristics of the screen used. (Courtesy Modern Photography)

Figure-Ground Enhancement

An interesting example of figure-ground enhancement concerns the photographing of a sonar screen to detect the presence of submarines during World War II. The image of a submarine on the screen is dependent upon sound waves being reflected from the submarine. Since there are also other things in the water reflecting sound waves, a visual noise pattern is displayed on the screen which obscures the image of the submarine making the signal-to-noise ratio too low to detect it. The following simple and ingenious technique was used to solve the problem. A series of pictures was made over a given time period. These pictures were then superimposed and viewed. Since the noise pattern on the sonar screen was random, the effect of superposition of the pictures was to average out the noise. The image of the submarine was not random and was, therefore, enhanced. The total effect was an increase in the signal-to-noise ratio; a much improved figure-ground; a detectable submarine.

A photographer continually uses the concept of figure-ground in making pictures, although he may use terms such as focus, filter, contrast, resolving power, graininess, and the like to describe it. By selectively focusing his camera he chooses what is figure (in focus) and what is ground. By using a yellow filter over his camera when photographing a scene in which there are white clouds against a blue sky, he improves the contrast and the clouds are more emphasized (better figure). By using different grades of printing paper when printing a negative, he alters the contrast of a picture and improves the figure. Shadow areas in a print that have little or no detail are improved by *dodging* (selectively holding back the light) while printing the negative.

Figure-ground provides another way of looking at resolving power. What is the greatest distance you can get from a picket fence to photograph it and still be able to see each picket distinctly in the photograph? This is a measure of resolving power. When you can no longer distinguish the pickets you have lost figure-ground.

Photographers who do not pay attention to the background when photographing people or objects often find that, in the two-dimensional frame of a photograph, depth is collapsed and ground sometimes becomes figure. This effect is seen in photographs of people with fenceposts growing from their heads.

Nonvisual Figure-Ground

The concept of figure-ground is not limited to visual experiences but can be applied to all sensory experiences.

SOUND

You can demonstrate the concept of figure-ground with sound by talking to a friend in a normal voice when there are other sounds in the background; for example, at a cocktail party, in a noisy restaurant, or on a busy street corner. Usually it is possible to carry on a conversation. Your voice is figure (signal) and the other sounds are background (noise).

TACTILITY

Run your fingers over a surface of some textured object. What you feel is figure, the information that tells you the texture of the surface. The reading of Braille depends on feeling the raised dots and determining their configuration.

TASTE

Carefully sip from a glass of quality wine and attend to the variety of tastes and smells (one at a time) that you can distinguish, such as sweet, mild, flowery, etc. Professional winetasters have their own vocabulary—delicate, noble, soft, foxy, mousy, mellow, elegant, robust, simple, and complex.

SMELL

In a room with many different odors you will undoubtedly smell that which is strongest or, depending upon your own individual set, that which is least or most familiar. In so doing you are distinguishing figure from ground.

Since all of our senses are tied into the same central system (information processing center), it is not surprising that a concept such as figure-ground should be valid for all senses.

Figure-ground plays an important part in our daily lives. For example, when you purchase any item, be it a home or a camera, your choice is pretty much determined by what you are looking for. If you are looking for style when you buy a camera, that becomes figure and you choose on the basis of style or size, weight, lens, gimmick, or whatever you determine is important (figure). A husband and wife, looking over a furnished model home, will often disagree on the home. A possible reason is that one may be looking at the quality of construction (figure) and the other at overall design as enhanced by the attractive furnishings. Florists arranging flowers realize that the space between flowers is as important to the overall effect as the flowers themselves. Portrait photographers and cosmetologists use their techniques to accentuate the positive features in a face and eliminate the negative. Many other examples are possible. A special field of psychology looks upon certain mental disorders as the inability of a person to distinguish figure from ground in everyday experiences. Part of the therapy is directed toward helping the patient make these distinctions. The concept of figure-ground enters into most aspects of our daily living.

VIEWFINDER CAMERA

SINGLE REFLEX CAMERA

Viewing system as figure. In choosing a camera in a particular price range, look for one in which the viewing system makes it easy for you to see the picture, otherwise you will miss much of the fun in making photographs. Look for a viewing system that is big and bright and makes focusing easy. Two basic types of viewing systems are shown above.

4. Gestalt Laws

The Gestalt psychologists were especially interested in figure-ground relationships and in the things that help a person to see objects as patterns or good figure. They suggested a number of principles, but we shall concern ourselves with four only:

1. Proximity.
2. Similarity.
3. Continuity.
4. Closure.

These four Gestalt principles or laws are important to conceptualize, for if a photographer knows how a person most probably organizes or groups visual elements when looking at pictures, he can then arrange the elements to favor or disfavor certain groupings.

Proximity

The closer two or more visual elements are, the greater is the probability that they will be seen as a group or pattern. Look at the circles in Fig. 18. Each configuration of circles in A, B, or C can be seen as forming a square. Within the square in B, the circles are closer together horizontally than vertically and, therefore, are seen as groups of horizontal rows or as a horizontal movement. It is difficult to see them otherwise. The effect can be enhanced by moving the horizontal circles closer together. Move the circles to a position where they are physically or psychologically (visual resolution) touching and you would see a line. The circles in C are seen as vertical columns or movements since they are closer together in the vertical direction. Because the circles in A are at equal distances, they are not easily seen as vertical or horizontal.

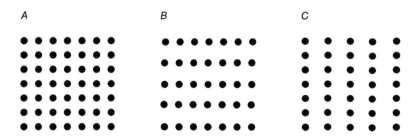

Figure 18.

Organization of visual elements according to the law of proximity.

The circles in Fig. 18A, B, and C demonstrate that, using the same visual elements and simply changing their proximity to each other, a viewer will group them in different ways. As an exercise you might try rearranging the space between the circles so that a person sees groupings of circles in a slant direction. Try some other arrangements. To test your success, have your friends look at the arrangements.

SPACE IS THREE-DIMENSIONAL

Moving the circles in Fig. 18 closer to each other horizontally facilitated a horizontal grouping of circles; closer proximity vertically facilitated a vertical grouping. If the circles were in a three-dimensional array one could move them into greater proximity in the third dimension and facilitate grouping in terms of depth. This is exactly what happens, for example, when photographs are taken of people with no consideration for the background. Since a photograph is a two-dimensional representation, objects in three-dimensional space are brought into closer proximity and tend to be seen as one group. The problem increases as the focal length of the lens increases.

Proximity of objects in space, then, influences the way in which we group visual elements. Since space is three-dimensional, *think* three-dimensionally when preparing to take a picture. Look at Figs. 19, 20, and 21, which illustrate the ways in which objects arrange themselves:

a) side by side;
b) up and down;
c) front to back.

Figure 19. Proximity facilitates grouping side by side.

Figure 20. Proximity facilitates grouping up and down.

Figure 21. Proximity facilitates grouping front to back.

***PROXIMITY
AND COMBINATION
PRINTING***

Combination printing of negatives to bring visual elements from the different negatives into greater proximity facilitates their grouping and association (Fig. 22).

by Jerry Uelsmann

Figure 22.   Combination printing facilitates grouping.

FOLD-IN

A novel example of the application of proximity is the fold-in feature that appears regularly in *Mad* comics (Fig. 23). Before the reader folds the page so that positions A and B meet, he is usually unable to predict exactly what the new picture will be. All the pictorial information is present before the page is folded, but section A and section B are not in close proximity, so it is difficult to group the information into one picture. It is interesting to cut out strip B and slowly slide it to the left until you are able to predict what new picture will result when strip B combines with A.

Another way to facilitate the grouping of the pictorial information to the left of A and to the right of B is to remove the unnecessary information between A and B. It is included only to distract the viewer and is similar to noise in a communication system. To experience what would happen if you removed this visual noise, cut out a strip of plain paper the width of A-B and use it as an overlay.

A   *FOLD THIS SECTION OVER LEFT*   ◀ B   *FOLD BACK SO "A" MEETS "B"*

Figure 23. The proximity of sections A and B determines the ease in which the two sections will be grouped. (Courtesy MAD, © 1972 by E. C. Publications, Inc.)

**WORDS
AND NUMBERS**

Spacing between letters or numbers plays an important role in what is seen. Read the words below:

FAT   HER
HAT   RED
PEN   TAX

Did you read them as six separate words or as three?

Some time ago while browsing in a bookstore I noticed a book with this title:

SUPER-
VISION

I was delighted and excited to have found a new book dealing with extraordinary visual phenomena. A scanning of it was disappointing, however, for it proved to be a business book on supervision. I wondered whether the publisher realized what he had done by the particular arrangement of the title on his book cover.

Do the six numbers listed below mean anything to you?

362436

If not, rewrite the numbers leaving an extra space between the second and third numbers and between the fourth and fifth numbers. Does the spacing force you to group the numbers differently and change your perceptual experience?

Consider the critical nature of horizontal space between the visual elements *1* and *3* shown in Fig. 24.

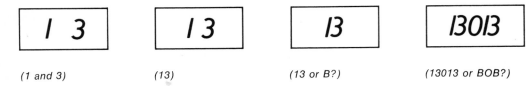

(1 and 3)   (13)   (13 or B?)   (13013 or BOB?)

Figure 24. Although the visual elements are the same (1 and 3), their changing proximity can cause different perceptions and perhaps even uncertainty and ambiguity.

**TEMPORAL
PROXIMITY**

Proximity is not limited to the spatial arrangement of things. It also applies to the temporal arrangement of events. Things that occur close together in time will tend to be grouped together. Tell someone that you are going to spell a word aloud and that you want him to name the word. He will think it an easy task, and indeed it is, unless you pause between certain letters. The word is CHO PHO USE. Spell the word aloud in groups of three letters. It will be difficult to name the word unless the listener rehearses the letters given him so that the pauses between all letters are equal. This experiment has been tried with a number of people, and few are able to name the word without mentally rehearsing it or writing it so that it can be reconstructed without time delays.

Music provides yet another example of the importance of proximity to perception. The sound of middle C on a piano represents a frequency of 262 cycles per second. If the frequency is increased, the sound vibrations occur closer together in time and the acoustical experience is an increase in pitch.

Motion picture and television editing requires careful placement of frames so that their projection in time will favor grouping. One of the major reasons for editing is to facilitate the perceptual grouping of elements that occur in time and space. Events that occur close together in time and space tend to be grouped together.

Apply the Gestalt law of proximity to the arrangements of things you photograph and design and you can encourage people to see the relationships you want them to see. For the most part they will be unaware of how you arranged the visual elements, since spatial and temporal proximity are natural ways for us to group things. When things are experienced as grouped, we see the whole and not the individual elements that make up the whole.

**PROXIMITY
AND LEARNING**

Information presented side by side or in the same time frame facilitates learning. Not only do we tend to group events that occur close together; we also tend to associate them and make comparisons. This has always been used effectively in advertising and, occasionally, in teaching. Fig. 25A and B show examples of proximity in learning and in advertising.

It is important to note that the eye can make the most critical judgments of whether two visual stimuli are the same or different when the stimuli occur side by side in space. Visual instruments such as densitometers and colorimeters operate on this principle. When you are trying to make a better photographic print you usually compare it side by side with your previous print or some reference print. One of the most difficult tasks for a photofinisher is to print your color negative so that the print matches a print you have received earlier. When you get the new print and compare it with the previous one you will invariably find differences. One of the first things students learn in color printing is that it is easier to get acceptance of a color print when it is not compared with another.

Many photographers are not clear about the relationships that exist among some very familiar terms used in photography: *stops, factors, neutral density filter*, and *exponents*. A photographer usually talks about changing exposure by stops. He realizes that a 1-stop change means an increase or decrease by a factor of 2. How is this related to exponents to the base 2 and to ND filters in 0.30 increments? Making a table in which exponents, factors, stops, and ND filters are in close proximity helps one to see and remember the relationships.

RELATIONSHIPS

Factors	Exponents (Base 2)	Stops	Neutral Density Filter
1	2^0	0	0.00
2	2^1	1	0.30
4	2^2	2	0.60
8	2^3	3	0.90
16	2^4	4	1.20

Note that stops are exponents to the base 2. Factors are the numbers that result from raising base 2 to a power (exponent). The factor increases by 2 each time the exponent increases by 1. The relationships between exponents (base 2), factors, and stops seem logical, but the increments for ND filters do not. The reason is that density values are based on exponents to base 10. It can be somewhat confusing, but all you need remember is that a density change of 0.30 is 1 stop (0.15 is a 1/2-stop change). Mathematically, $2^1 = 10^{0.30} = 2$. Density values for *all* filters are log 10 values, and logarithms are exponents.

Whatever favors organization and comparison will also favor learning, retention, and recall. Thus the law of proximity is equivalent to what educators call association by contiguity. In terms of information processing, pictures presented side by side and in proximity require less memory storage and retrieval. Pictures presented in a *time* sequence rely more on memory, and the longer the time delay the more probable the loss of information or distortion of information in memory.

NEGATIVE   *POSITIVE*

Figure 25A. Proximity facilitates learning by comparison. Note how the white shadows in the negative and the black shadows in the positive affect the design imprint. In one case the imprint looks raised and in the other depressed. Rotate the book 180 degrees and observe what happens. Make comparisons at different angles. At what angle does the imprint reverse itself?

SUPER TAKUMAR LENS   SUPER-MULTI-COATED TAKUMAR LENS

Figure 25B. Proximity facilitates comparisons in advertising.

Photograph by James Katzel (Courtesy Honeywell Photographic Products)

PROXIMITY AND AREA

The smaller an area of space, the greater the probability that it will be seen as figure. This statement is similar to the one made about proximity. Every area is bounded by an edge or line. The greater the proximity of these edges or lines, the greater the probability that the area within the lines will be seen as figure. This was demonstrated earlier in the equivocal fence diagram. Fig. 26 shows how proximity of lines and area are related and how they facilitate the selective segregation of the smaller visual segments from the larger so that the smaller segments are seen as figure. Notice also that it is much easier to see the smaller segments as figure in the middle illustration than in the other two. This demonstrates the importance of contrast and how it can be used, along with area, to increase or decrease the ease with which certain visual patterns are seen as figure. An example of the effective use of area and contrast in the design of graphics and in photographs are shown in Figs. 27 and 28.

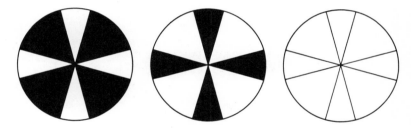

Figure 26.

Proximity of lines or edges and area are related. The closer the lines or edges, the smaller the area, and therefore the greater the probability it will be seen as figure.
It is easier to see the smaller segments as figure against the larger segments as ground.

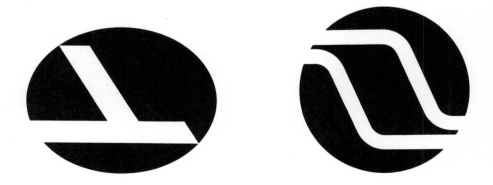

EASTERN AIRLINES   NORTHWEST ORIENT AIRLINES

Figure 27. Area and contrast play an important role in the design of graphics.

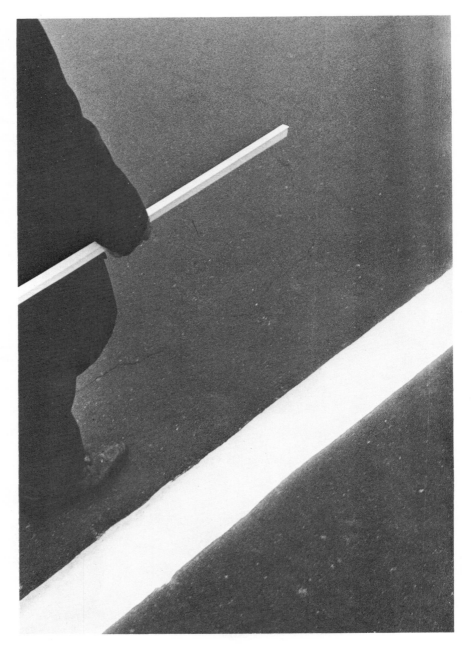

from DEJA-VU by Ralph Gibson

Figure 28. Area and contrast play a very important role in photographic design.
(© Lustrum Press)

AREA

Many examples of area can be found in advertising. Fig. 29A shows effective use of the fact that smaller areas are seen more readily as figure; Fig. 29B shows a total unawareness of this fact and leads to confusion. Visually, the smaller area calls attention to the hours from 6 to 10. Verbally, your attention is called to the hours from 10 to 6.

Figure 29A.

Area used effectively.

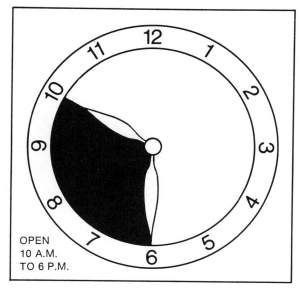

Figure 29B.

Area used ineffectively.

**AREA
AND CONTRAST**

Black on white provides a good level of visual contrast. The result is a high signal-to-noise ratio—a strong figure-ground. What is seen as figure, however, depends not only on contrast but also on area. In Fig. 30A the areas of the black bars and white bars are the same; it is equally probable that either will be seen as figure. In Fig. 30B, "reading" from top to bottom, figure evolves from a black line to a white line as area changes. Note, however, that about midway both the black and white bars are of equal area and there is a perceptual situation similar to A. Another example of the visual relationship between area and contrast is the halftone graphic arts screen shown in Fig. 31. "Reading" from left to right, figure changes from a black dot to a white dot.

Many other factors, of course, will influence what a person sees as figure—things such as shape, texture, color, closed areas vs. open areas, pattern, expectancy, etc. Figs. 30 and 31 emphasize two important variables in design and perception: area and contrast. And other variables to these illustrations, such as color, and what is seen as figure can change.

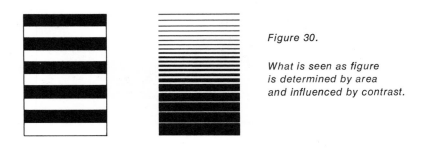

Figure 30.

*What is seen as figure
is determined by area
and influenced by contrast.*

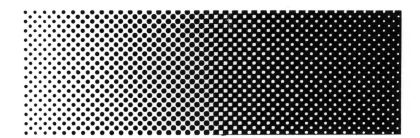

Figure 31.

A halftone screen in which small dot areas, whether black or white, are seen as figure.

Similarity   *Visual elements that are similar (in shape, size, color, etc.) tend to be seen as related.* When we see things that are related we naturally group them and therefore see them as patterns. This is readily observable in Fig. 32. The overall configuration for A, B, and C remains square, but B is now seen as having horizontal rows of alternating circles and squares and C is seen as having vertical columns of alternating circles and squares. Since all the visual elements in Fig. 32A are similar and have the same proximity, no patterns are seen within the array. Note that the proximity of the visual elements in B and C remains constant but that the grouping of these elements in alternating vertical and horizontal directions is based on the similarity of circles or squares. This demonstrates the influence of similar elements in the way we see and group things. It also suggests that similarity can be a stronger force than proximity in perceptual grouping. Further examples are presented in Fig. 33.

A   B   C

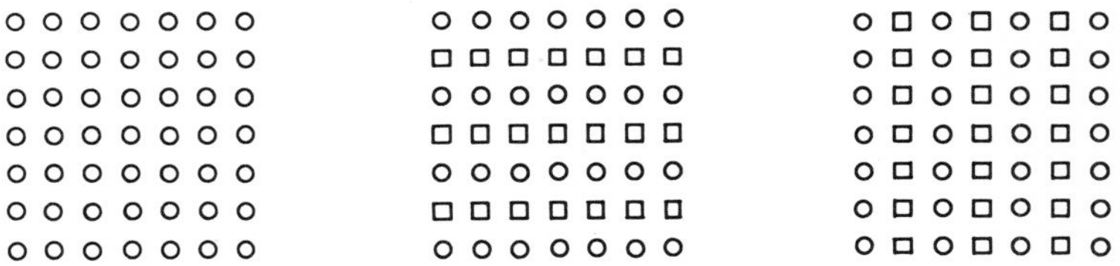

Figure 32.

Organization of visual elements according to the law of similarity (shape).

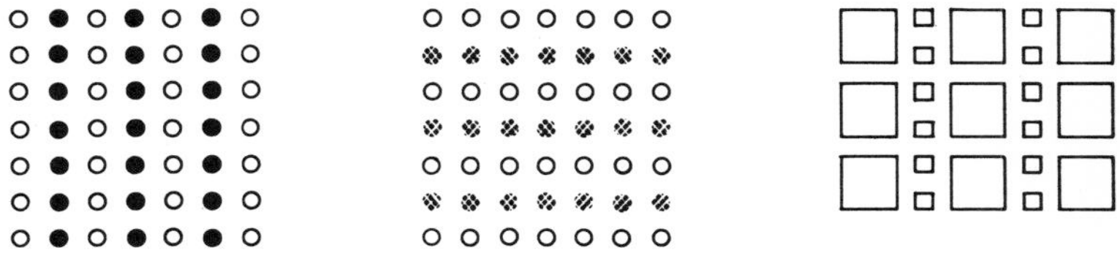

COLOR SIMILARITY

Visual elements that are similar in color* (hue, chroma, value) are readily grouped.

TEXTURE SIMILARITY

Visual elements that are similar in texture are readily grouped.

SIZE SIMILARITY

Visual elements that are of similar size are readily grouped.

*Black is a color that has zero hue and chroma but has value (brightness **or** lightness).

Figure 33.

Further examples of the ease with which similar visual elements are grouped.

Refer to Fig. 26 and note how natural it is to group the four small (or large) pie-shaped segments together and how extremely difficult it is to group dissimilar segments such as a small segment and two large segments. There are many different patterns that one could abstract from Fig. 26 by various groupings of small and large pie-shaped segments. It is relatively easy to do this by using pencil and paper but extremely difficult to do by just looking. Try it!

SIMILARITY OF SHAPE

Visual elements that have similar shapes such as those shown in the skeleton of a leaf tend to be grouped together (Fig. 34). Because of the similarity and proximity of the curved lines, they are easily grouped together to form a pattern. Such repetition of similar lines can be thought of as a visual beat, a visual counterpart of the rhythm that is associated with motion and sound.

Fig. 35 shows the effective use of similar shapes and forms in facilitating grouping.

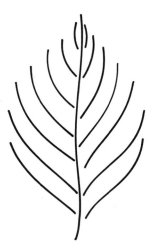

Figure 34.

Grouping of visual elements having similar shapes.
(Curved lines are actual tracings from a leaf.)

by Scott Calder

Figure 35. Similar faces. (Courtesy Ilford Inc., a Ciba-Geigy Company, Paramus, N.J.)

PAINTING

The familiar painting *American Gothic* by Grant Wood provides some interesting observations on similarity (Fig. 36). Perhaps the most obvious is the shape of the three-pronged pitchfork and the "three prong" design in the man's coverall just to the right of the pitchfork. One can also find the curved shape of the fork rhythmically repeated several places; the upper part of the woman's apron, and the white collars and chin lines of the wife and husband. The facial expressions of the man and woman show very similar indentations under the nose and lips.

If one assumes that the pitchfork is symbolic of Satan then other "tridents" can be found in the painting:

a) the three vertical stripes in the man's shirt group with the three prong design in the coverall;
b) both faces are shaded in such a way that it is easy to group the nose and the area below it into the center prong of a trident (the outer prongs being the facial contour); and
c) the small cactus plant at the left side of the painting.

If such symbolic assumptions are valid then the expressions on the people in the picture take on new meanings and one can understand why this classic portrait of rural Americans precipitated an uproar among Midwesterners when it was first exhibited at the Art Institute of Chicago in 1930.

by Grant Wood

Figure 36. American Gothic. (Courtesy the Art Institute of Chicago)

**SIMILARITY OF
SIZE, POSITION,
AND SHAPE**

In Fig. 37 the positions of the hands, fingers, and pens are similar, as are the size and shape of the pens and the angles at which they are held. The photographer has been careful to show the same side of both pens. Even the shadows from the pen points are similar. In addition, the pens are in close proximity. Similarity of visual elements and proximity facilitate grouping.

Figure 37. Size, position, and shape similarity. (Courtesy Parker Pen Co.)

SIMILARITY AND PROXIMITY

A photographer was taking routine pictures of a sidewalk exhibition of paintings when he recorded the unusual photo shown in Fig. 38. When asked if he saw the similarity between foreground and background when he took the picture, he commented, "It happened so quickly I didn't have time to think—I just saw something unusual that caught my eye and I instantly tripped the shutter."

Note the similar positioning of the arm of the woman in the chair and the arm of Mr. Nixon in the upper painting. You have probably also noticed that the crossed leg of the woman in the chair has the right shape and position to be grouped as part of the blouse of the woman in the lower painting. The proximity of the two portraits and the woman in the chair, along with the similarities mentioned, facilitates a grouping that generates a geometric form.

by Robert W. Agostino

Figure 38.

Similarity and proximity.

**SIMILARITY
OF MEANING**

Photographers and artists sometimes use symbolic associations to provide similarity and grouping. Fig. 39 shows how an advertiser used a photograph of a cat sleeping curled up alongside an air conditioner that has a unit similar in shape to that of the cat; this similarity of shapes facilitates grouping, which in turn enhances association between the familiar quietness of the sleeping cat and the implied quietness of the air conditioner.

In Fig. 40 the photographer has captured a moment from our time and challenges us to relate it to a moment in time some 1900 years ago. He assumes that we have seen paintings and statues of the crucifixion of Jesus and that we retain in visual memory a cross and a limp figure of a man. By using similar design elements the photographer facilitates our grouping of these two events (the photograph and what is in memory). When this occurs the photograph takes on a much deeper meaning and feeling.

*Figure 39. Similarity of shape and projected similarity of meaning.
(Courtesy York Division, Borg-Warner Corp.)*

by Bruce Davidson

Figure 40. One of a series of photographs taken in the East 100th Street area of New York City.

SYMMETRY   Symmetry can be considered a special case of similarity. Visual elements that are symmetrical provide for visual balance—for a "good gestalt." The more symmetrical an area is, the greater the tendency is to group it and see it as figure. Fig. 41 shows how one readily groups symmetrical shapes to see the vertical areas *1, 3,* and *5* as figure. It is extremely difficult to see vertical areas *2* and *4* as figure since their vertical boundaries are not symmetrical. The more symmetrical an area is the more readily it is seen as figure.

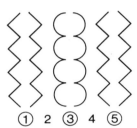

Figure 41. Symmetry facilitates grouping.

Fig. 41 represents a simple situation to illustrate the importance of symmetry to grouping. Much of what we encounter in life is in some way symmetrical. In the visual world, symmetry of line or shape is also accompanied by other things such as color, tone, texture, form, etc. Add any one of these things to Fig. 41 and the grouping can change. If, for example, the nonsymmetrical areas *2* and *4* are colored, they will group and the other areas will serve as ground. The same will happen if you simply close areas *2* and *4.*

Fig. 41, therefore, is highly abstract to emphasize the importance of symmetry of line to grouping. You usually do not encounter such a situation in photography except in photographic derivations in which color, tone, texture, etc. can be negated. You can, however, find examples of symmetry of line operating in designs and in sketches (Fig. 42).

Figure 42. Symmetry of line. Areas bounded by symmetrical lines are more readily grouped than those which are not.

**SIMILARITY
AND SYMMETRY**

Visual elements do not need to be symmetrical to be similar in shape, form, color, etc. However, when they are both similar and symmetrical they can, as shown in Fig. 43, provide a visual rhythm —a balanced, repetitive grouping. In terms of good organizational composition the photograph has the characteristics of simplicity, similarity, symmetry, balance, and stability. In terms of communications theory there is desirable redundancy. In the terms in which Henri Cartier-Bresson talks about photographs one might say that there is a "relationship of form" and "geometric pattern."

by Richard Avedon

Figure 43. Similarity and symmetry of form. (Art Director, William Taubin, Courtesy Doyle Dane Bernback Inc.)

**SYMMETRY AND
GRAPHIC SYMBOLS**

Symmetry plays an important part in the graphic identifications used by many corporations. Note in Fig. 44 the visual balance provided by the symmetry of the visual elements. Note also the proximity of the visual elements and how proximity and symmetry work together to facilitate the grouping of the visual elements into a whole visual unit—into a gestalt.

You have probably also observed the strong figure-ground relationships present in these logos.

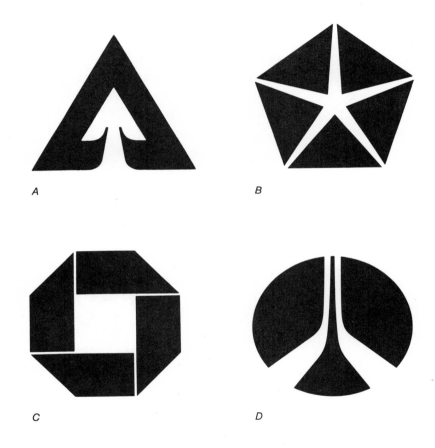

A

B

C

D

Figure 44.

Examples of symmetry in the design of graphics:

*A. Weyerhauser Company; B. Chrysler Corporation;
C. Chase Manhattan; D. Rockwell International.*

Continuity

Visual elements that require the fewest number of interruptions will be grouped to form continuous straight or curved lines. If you refer to the array of small circles in Fig. 32A and consider all the possible lines or shapes that could be generated from such a 7 × 7 array of circles, it becomes apparent that man's visual process seeks simple lines and shapes—those that require the least change or interruption in the visual experience. If the array of circles in Fig. 32A were an array of electric lights, and if each light were wired to go on or off independently, we would have a system for generating just about any line or shape we might desire. The signs around such places as Times Square, Picadilly Circus, and the Ginza are examples. (When all the lights are on or off we have, however, a situation similar to Fig. 32A.) A television screen is, in a way, similar to such signs, for it has four million little lights (phosphor dots). Analogies could be made to other display systems such as the halftone dot matrix in graphic arts.

Refer now to Fig. 45 and try to remember the first thing that you saw. Was it a pair of *X*'s? Seeing a pair of *X*'s would require the fewest interruptions or changes. Seeing a diamond is also relatively simple. Both the *X*'s and the diamond are familiar and require few visual changes. The diamond, in addition, is a closed figure and this facilitates its perception. We shall be discussing this later when we talk about closure. If you look hard enough you can see other familiar figures, perhaps a *W*, an *M*, or a *V*. The letters *W, M*, and *V* are harder to see because they require more visual changes. Put differently, it is easier to see the slanting lines as continuous; harder to see them as discontinuous.

Figure 45.

Organization of visual elements according to the law of continuity.

FLAGS

The Union Flag and Jack shown in Fig. 46 provides an interesting example of continuation. It is easy to see a cross and an *X*. The cross is continuous, and it would be extremely difficult to see it otherwise. The *X*, however, is discontinuous but, because of the arrangement of visual line elements, it is relatively easy to see as continuous. It is interesting to note that this Union Flag is a combination of national emblems of England, Scotland, and Northern Ireland.

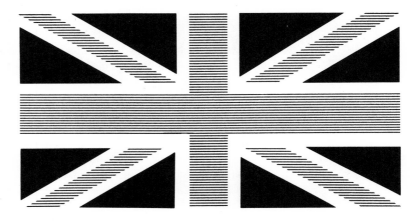

Figure 46. The Union Flag of the United Kingdom.

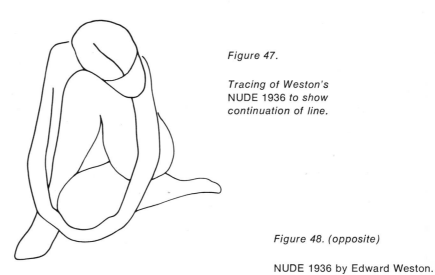

Figure 47.

Tracing of Weston's NUDE 1936 to show continuation of line.

Figure 48. (opposite)

NUDE 1936 by Edward Weston.

CONTINUATION OF LINE

Edward Weston's *Nude 1936* has become a classic photograph (Fig. 48). Much can be said about it, not the least of which is that it is an excellent photographic example of the importance of continuation of line (Fig. 47).

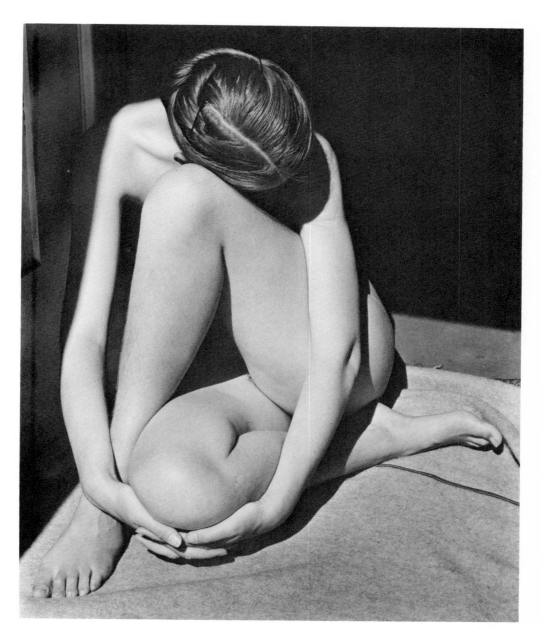

**CONTINUATION
AND PROXIMITY**

In Fig. 49 two separate patterns are seen, but as the lines in A are brought into closer proximity, the curved shapes group into a continuous sinusoidal line (B).

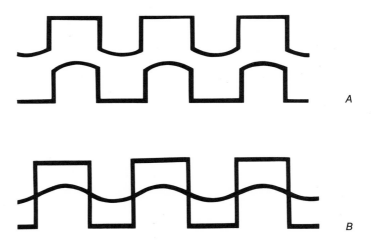

Figure 49. Proximity facilitates continuation.

LAYOUT

In advertising layout, continuation and other Gestalt Laws can be used to facilitate grouping. This can serve to provide interest in the advertisement, since the viewer is given the opportunity to participate in the grouping. The closure that results provides for a rhythmic redundancy (Fig. 50).

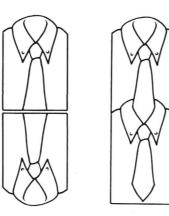

Figure 50.

Possible layouts for a shirt and tie advertisement.

SKETCHES   Fig. 51 is a detail of a pencil drawing by William Blake. It shows
an old man seated with a book between his knees arguing with
two men in monkish habits. Note the careful placement of the
monk's extended finger, which groups easily with the curved cowl
of the monk. Note also that the tips of the extended fingers continue on to group with the cowl of the other monk.

by William Blake

Figure 51.

*Detail of Historical Scene, unidentified. (Courtesy National Gallery
of Art, Washington, D. C., Lessing J. Rosenwald Collection)*

TYPOGRAPHY   Type comes in many different styles. One style that has dominated printing for many years is the serif type style (Fig. 52A). One possible reason for its dominance might be that it provides a "good" gestalt. In the example below, the serif type letters in the upper word *WINE* seem to group more naturally than the letters in the lower word *WINE.* The terminal strokes (serifs) on the letters provide better visual continuity. Fig. 52B shows a novel example of the use of continuity in typography.

Figure 52A. The upper word WINE is an example of serif type style. The letters group easier than they do in the lower word WINE.

Figure 52B. Continuation can be used to provide some interesting effects with printed words.

**CONTINUITY
OF SEQUENCES**

Motion pictures (whether the medium is film or video tape) can be thought of as a sequence of visual images that vary in their spatial as well as temporal arrangement.

The same can be said for still pictures that are sequenced in a spatial array, for as a person views each picture he is doing so in a time frame (Fig. 53). One difference between motion pictures and still pictures that have been arranged in sequence is that in the latter, far fewer pictures per event are represented. Jumping abruptly from one scene to the next, or from one train of thought to another, causes one to perceive the events as unrelated. What precedes or follows a frame or a picture influences the perception of it. There are situations, of course, when creating just such an experience—a disruption, a dissonance—is desired. But for the most part, the attempt is to provide a smooth and continuous (both in space and time) transition (Fig. 53). Dissolves, fades in or out of focus, wipes, and similar techniques are designed to enhance this transition.

When we try to represent visual and auditory experiences through the use of sight and sound media it is imperative that a good continuity of events be established. This is the main purpose of script writing, storyboarding, and editing film, video tape, audio tape, and written texts.

WOMEN JUMPING OVER CHAIRS—20 LATERAL VIEWS by E. Muybridge

Figure 53. Sequence still photography. (Courtesy George Eastman House)

Closure

Nearly complete familiar lines and shapes are more readily seen as complete (closed) than incomplete. In Fig. 54 the viewer groups the visual elements to see a triangle, not three unrelated lines; a circle, not a series of dots. The proximity and similarity of the visual elements are important in order to facilitate this perception of a triangle and a circle as one seeks to establish a visual equilibrium—a balance, a closure.

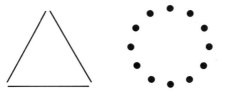

Figure 54.

Organization of visual elements according to the law of closure.

ARMY FLAG

The design of the five-star flag for a general of the United States Army provides a very effective example of closure (Fig. 55). A careful look at the area within the five stars causes one to see a pentagon shape. The physical shape formed by the edges of the stars is not continuous, but is perceived as continuous because the Gestalt law of closure is operating. Other Gestalt laws are also operating to facilitate this perception:

a) proximity—the closeness of the stars;
b) similarity—all the stars are of the same size, shape, and color (white); and
c) continuation—the orientation of the stars is such that straight continuous lines are formed from each of the five pentagon apexes.

Figure 55.

General of the Army Flag. A pentagon shape can be seen when closure within the star is made.

Presidential flags further illustrate the interdependence of the Gestalt laws (Fig. 56A and B). Both the presidential and vice-presidential flag symbols have visual elements (stars) that can be grouped together to form a circle. It is only with the presidential flag symbols, however, that the stars are seen as forming a continuous line describing a circle. Closure to form a circle of stars provides a good Gestalt. The stroboscopic photograph of a golfer by Dr. Harold Edgerton provides a multiplicity of visual elements that are easily grouped into a spiral shape (Fig. 57).

Figure 56.

A. Symbol of the flag of the Vice President of the USA.

NON-CLOSURE—although the 13 stars are the same, they are not in proper proximity to allow easy closure of the visual elements. It is extremely difficult to see a circle even though the stars are laid out in the form of a circle.

B. Symbol of the flag of the President of the USA.

CLOSURE—the proximity of the stars and the similarity of their orientation and shapes provide for continuation and closure. The 50 stars form a circle.

by Harold Edgerton

Figure 57. A shell-like spiral design emerges as the visual elements are grouped.

CLOSURE AND OTHER GESTALT PRINCIPLES AT WORK

The famous photograph by Bresson (Fig. 58) provides, among other things, an excellent example of closure. As the man leaps from the wooden ladder the position of his legs forms a sharp angle, which is reflected in the water. The reflected image of the feet is in close proximity to the real image but not quite touching. This is especially true for the heel of the front foot. Although the feet (visual elements) are not touching, they are close enough to allow a closure that produces a geometric shape, a pentagon. When the white shape of a pentagon is seen, it immediately becomes *figure*. You can also see this pentagon shape as the head of an arrow pointing forward. This emphasizes the movement of the man. Carrying this thought a step further, the wooden ladder is in the right position and proximity to be grouped and become part of the arrow. You can see other Gestalt principles in operation and the way in which they facilitate this grouping. The reflected image provides similarity and symmetry. The white water and black outline of the man's legs provide a strong contrast—a strong figure-ground.

PARIS, 1932
by Henri Cartier Bresson

Figure 58.
Closure and other Gestalt laws provide structure in this famous photograph.

PROXIMITY, SIMILARITY, CONTINUATION, AND CLOSURE

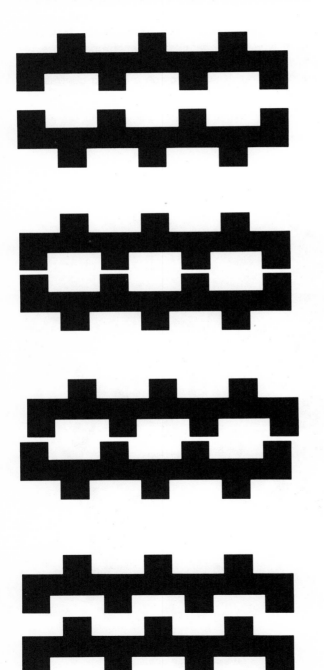

Figure 59.

A. The distance between the two sets of alternating black squares is too great to allow grouping.

B. The two sets of alternating black squares are close enough to be grouped so that a closure is formed when the three white squares are seen.

C. The two sets of alternating black squares are in proper proximity, but their position is offset and interferes with the continuity of the edges. Grouping and closure are denied.

D. Although proximity and position are correct there is no grouping because of the dissimilarity of tone (value).

...SED AREAS

Areas with closed contours are more readily seen than areas with open contours. The closed areas *2* and *5* are easier to see than the open areas *1, 3, 4*, and *6*, even though the jagged lines are all similar and are in the same proximity to each other (Fig. 60).

One of the reasons the letter M shown earlier in Fig. 8 is so difficult to see is because the area is open, not closed. The arrows, being closed, are readily seen as figure. (Refer to Fig. 61 for a photographic example.)

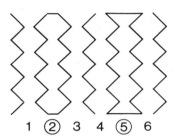

Figure 60.

Closed areas are more easily seen as figure.

detail from
CORSETS, PARIS, 1910
by Eugene Atget

Figure 61.

The corsets represent areas of closed contour and are readily seen as figure. Note also that the symmetrical ground areas between corsets are more easily seen than the nonsymmetrical areas. (Refer to Figure 41.) (Courtesy Museum of Modern Art)

**RESOLVING
POWER TARGETS**

The widths of the black bars in a resolving power target are exactly the same as the white spaces between them (Fig. 62). The length of the black bars is definite because they are closed areas, whereas the white spaces are not even seen as bars because they are open areas. To see the white spaces as white bars, one has to provide for closure. You can do this by simply drawing a line to enclose the three bars into a square.

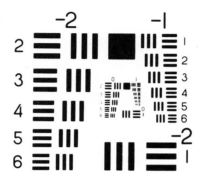

Figure 62.

The closed black bars on a resolving power target are easily seen as figure.

**SINGLE
CONTOUR LINE**

Earlier in the book a single contour line was used to show a figure-ground boundary. This line, with some effort, could be seen as belonging to the face of an old man or to part of the face and body of a woman. The perception of one over the other can be controlled by enclosing the single contour line (Fig. 63). In this way a photographer can manipulate visual elements so that perception of what is to be communicated is more certain.

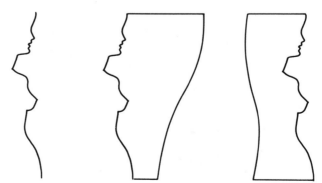

Figure 63.

Profile of an old man or head and torso of a woman? Closed areas are more readily seen as figures. Contrasting the enclosed areas by darkening them makes them even easier to see as figures.

**William Henry
Jackson**

A photograph that shows excellent geometric form and nicely demonstrates the operative Gestalt laws is Henry Jackson's photograph of three American Indian women and a child (Fig. 64).

Figure 64.

Three North American Indian women photographed by Henry Jackson. (Courtesy Smithsonian Institution National Anthropological Archives, Bureau of American Ethnology Collection)

GEOMETRIC FORM The positions of the faces of the three women are such that they are easily grouped to form an equilateral triangle (A). A similar but inverted equilateral triangle could also be formed by grouping the faces of the two seated women and the young child (B). Other groupings are also possible, such as the diamond shape as the foot position of the child is grouped with the faces of the three women (C).

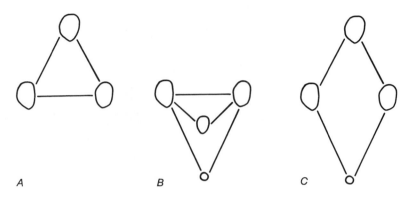

A   B   C

Figure 64.

The grouping of the various visual elements into triangular shapes might be analyzed in this way:

1. *Proximity.* The faces of the three women are in exact position to form a triangle. The two who are seated are at eye level with each other. They form a base line for the standing woman's head as one apex, or the baby's face or toes as another.
2. *Similarity.* Grouping into a series of triangular shapes is facilitated by the similarity of the shapes of the faces, the facial features, hair style, and expression.
   In addition, the overall forms of each woman and of the child are triangular, providing a multiplicity of this geometric shape. This multiplicity or repetition of form provides a visual rhythm or redundancy that enhances grouping.
3. *Continuity.* The outer shape of the women provides visual line elements that are close enough and in proper position to be grouped as continuous (D). Another example of continuity can be seen in the striped blanket of the standing woman. Jackson must have arranged the blanket carefully so that there would be continuity of stripes and so that they would form inverted triangular shapes.
4. *Closure.* One example of closure, of course, is the grouping of faces to form stable shapes such as triangles. Other examples are the ease with which one sees closed areas, such as those white and black stripes that do not blend in with the background.
5. *Figure-Ground.* You have perhaps noticed that Jackson was careful to move one of the hanging, light colored dress pieces and place it behind the head of the standing women so as to provide a good figure-ground in a critical picture area.

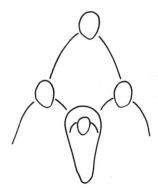

D

Camouflage   The art of camouflage is the art of deception. It involves the arrangement of visual elements in a way such that either they are grouped together and lose their individuality or they are blended into the background and lose their identity through a very poor figure-ground relationship (Fig. 65). Throughout this book the emphasis has been on the use of the Gestalt laws of perceptual organization to facilitate perception. The same laws can be used to facilitate the wrong perception.

If you want to hide something, manipulate it so that:

a) the object that is figure blends into the background; or
b) the object is put in close *proximity* to other objects that are *similar* in shape, size, color (hue, chroma, brightness); or
c) the object is in close proximity and aligned in such a way as to provide *continuity* of line.

These various arrangements will facilitate the grouping of visual elements and provide *closure.*

Figure 65. Faces embedded in clouds. (Courtesy Rochester Telephone Co.)

**Man as a
Participant**

Man derives satisfaction from being able to form a closure that allows him to become an active participant in the visual experience. The concept of closure is not restricted to vision. It is basic to our humanity—to the way we experience things. A variety of examples can be cited to illustrate this. The art of teaching, in part, consists of providing the learner with enough information organized in such a way that he can put it together, add the missing element, and discover for himself (closure) what the teacher wants him to experience. If you recited "Mary had a little lamb whose fleece was white as _____," it could be predicted that you would finish (closure) the nursery rhyme with the word *snow* (assuming that you know the rhyme).

Years ago when cake mixes were first marketed they were a dismal economic failure even though the product was of good quality and very convenient to use. Research studies determined that the failure was due, ironically, to the fact that the manufacturer had done everything but bake the cake. He had, in fact, made it too convenient to use. By changing the cake mix ingredients and making it necessary for the user to increase active participation by cracking, adding, and mixing an egg (closure), cake mixes became an almost instant success. Every artist who successfully paints or photographs a nude knows that, in part, what he excludes is as important as what he includes. The viewer is allowed the freedom to include—to participate—to form closure.

The lesson is simple. In any planned experience never deprive the participant of the opportunity to participate—to become involved. Raising questions throughout this book is a way of attempting to apply this rule.

Gestalt Laws as a Means

Knowledge of language, by itself, does not make one a great writer or poet. Knowledge of the Gestalt laws, in and by itself, does not assure a good picture any more than does knowledge of the photographic process or of sophisticated photographic equipment and materials. Some of the excellent photographs made in the early days of photography attest to this. It is not sufficient merely to know about something. You must be able to apply that knowledge skillfully. A good photograph is a result of knowledge and ability—of knowing and doing. Both can come through rigorous discipline and practice.

The Gestalt laws, therefore, are not an end in themselves, but merely a means to an end, a means of producing a good photograph. The laws, which might better be thought of as guiding principles, attempt to describe in a simple way how man segregates and groups visual information. These principles, then, can guide a photographer in creating pictures that facilitate visual communications.

A WORD OF CAUTION

The Gestalt laws of perceptual organization have been separated in this book for convenience; convenience in presentation and convenience in learning. You must not, however, think of them as separate, for they are related and work together to facilitate seeing. Visual elements that are close together, that are similar, that form a smooth contour and allow for closure can provide for a good picture.

Keep in mind, however, that there are many excellent pictures that do not conform to the Gestalt laws of perceptual organization. Examples of such pictures are those with strong emotional appeal and those which delve into the unconscious. Remember, too, that there is a flip side to the Gestalt laws. If you know how to arrange visual elements so that they are easy to group visually, you also know how to arrange them so that they are difficult to group. You may choose to do the latter in order to create a feeling of tension or dissonance in your photograph, to camouflage, or merely to force the viewer to look harder.

5. Prägnanz

The Gestalt laws of organization are one attempt to formulate a set of principles that seem to describe the way we segregate and group visual elements into patterns or units. The overall rationale for the reasons man organizes and groups information the way he does is explained, in part, by the law of Prägnanz, which was introduced by the founder of the Gestalt movement, Dr. Max Wertheimer. In the words of Koffka* the law of Prägnanz can be formulated like this: *"psychological organization will always be as "good" as the prevailing conditions allow."* Although the term *good* is not defined, it is associated with such properties as regularity, symmetry, simplicity, uniformity, and closure; in short, properties that minimize stress and maximize stability. Prevailing conditions refer to the stimulus pattern (Fig. 66). More broadly it refers to the perceptual environment.

*See References.

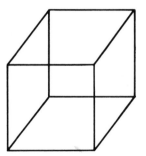

A. Stable as a three-dimensional pattern.

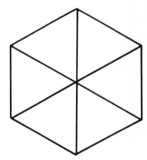

B. Stable as a two-dimensional pattern.

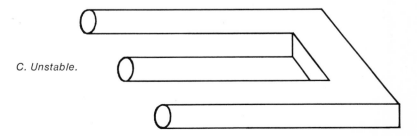

C. Unstable.

Figure 66.

Prevailing conditions influence psychological organization.

Seeing, however, involves more than just the stimulus pattern and environment. Much of what we see depends upon our past experiences (memory), our own personalities, and what we are looking for. This is why the same picture often gets a variety of responses from viewers. What a person experiences depends upon what he is *looking at* and what he is *looking for*, what is out there and what is in him.

Fig. 67 provides some insight into the complexity of what appears to be the simple process of seeing. What a person sees and experiences is called a *percept* (the product of perception, which is a process). What a person says he sees is a verbal attempt to describe a nonverbal experience. It is an attempt to verbalize a percept and often falls short. *Saying is not seeing.* What you see is not necessarily what you say. Psychologists and others still have no way of positively knowing a given person's percept and probably they never will. The percept is a result of interactions between the physical stimulus pattern and the unique psychological makeup of a person. No two people are completely alike, not even identical twins. To further complicate things, a person's psychological makeup varies from time to time and from place to place. The same cup of coffee will taste different in the morning from later in the day. Hot dogs taste differently at a football game than they do at home.

Many factors, therefore, influence what we experience and people will respond differently to what is "looked at." In spite of the differences among us there are some basic similarities, and these influence how we organize things. This, I believe, is the meaning of the law of Prägnanz. We tend to organize our world so that we can cope with it. We search for stability, meaning, balance, security, etc. We feel more comfortable when what we are looking at can be comprehended or experienced. If there is too much information presented at one time we either filter out some of it or simplify it by grouping or "chunking" it. If there is insufficient information we add to it to form a closure and maintain meaning. We strive to reduce tension and stress to obtain stability and equilibrium. The art and photography of mentally disturbed patients often reflects the chaotic conditions created by their illness or their inner struggle to achieve some sense of balance and stability.

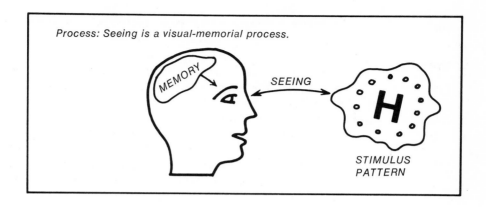

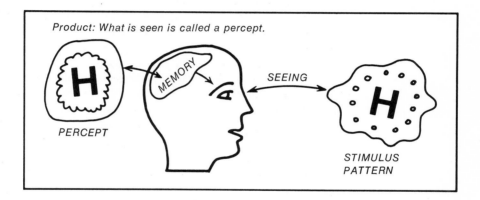

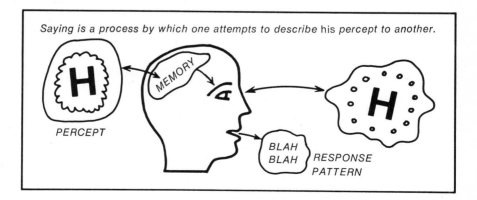

Figure 67. Seeing and saying are not the same.
Saying is a verbal attempt to describe a percept.

***Order
and
Complexity***

We defined Prägnanz' law as an overriding principle under which the Gestalt laws of perceptual organization operate. According to this principle, psychological organization or grouping of information is facilitated by such things as regularity, symmetry, simplicity, etc. The organization of information by a person is dependent upon the amount of information presented, which, in turn, depends on the redundancy and predictability of the various individual elements present within an array of information. In other words, if visual elements are well ordered there is a high degree of redundancy and, therefore, predictability. Psychological organization of the visual elements will be facilitated, but what is experienced (percept) could be quite boring.

The point is this: the Gestalt laws, if mechanistically applied in the practice of photography, art, design, or any other means of communications, might be technically correct, but the product could be monotonous and mundane. There may be no challenge for the person viewing what has been designed, no sense of excitement or of curiosity, no motivation to become involved. Too much has been done by the designer and there is little left for the viewer to add. Psychological organization is an active process from which a person derives pleasure and satisfaction. Too much order in a photograph or a design deprives a person of the creative act of participation. Some variation is needed to engage a person—"to add a little spice."

Rudolph Arnheim, who was a student of Max Wertheimer in the 1920s, eloquently describes the importance of variation in the design of things. He talks about order and complexity, defining order as "the degree and kind of lawfulness governing the relations among the parts of an entity" and complexity as "the multiplicity of the relationships among the parts of an entity." He then goes on to say:

Order and complexity are antagonistic, in that order tends to reduce complexity while complexity tends to reduce order. To create order requires not only rearrangement but in most cases also the elimination of what does not fit the principles determining the order. On the other hand, when one increases the complexity of an object, order will be harder to achieve.

Order and complexity, however, cannot exist without each other. Complexity without order produces confusion; order without complexity produces boredom. Although order is needed to cope with both the inner and outer world, man cannot reduce his experience to a network of neatly predictable connections without losing the stimulating riches and surprises of life. Being complexly designed, man must function complexly if he is to be fully himself; and to this end the setting in which he operates must be complex also. It has long been recognized that the great works of man combine high order with high complexity.*

*Rudolph Arnheim, *Psychology of Art* (Berkeley: University of California Press, 1972), p. 124.

Information Theory

There are alternate ways to describe the same experience. The Gestalt laws were formulated in the early 1900s to provide some principles of how man tends to group visual elements. In the mid-1900s visual elements were identified as informational elements, and the ways in which such elements were grouped could be described in terms of information or communication theory. The principal concepts are uncertainty and redundancy. The amount of information conveyed by what we see (percept), for example, depends upon the number of different ways in which visual elements can be grouped (uncertainty or alternatives). The more redundant the visual elements, the fewer the alternatives and the easier the grouping. One of the reasons why things that are symmetrical are so easy to see is that there is great redundancy of information. Information on any one side of the symmetrical figure is readily predictable from information on the opposite side. Symmetry is one of the things that provides for a "good" Gestalt —for Prägnanz. The graphic symbols used by many corporations and businesses are often symmetrical (Fig. 68). Such redundancy

Figure 68.

PURE WOOL ®   PURE WOOL ®

The Pure Wool mark provides a good gestalt. There is good figure-ground, regularity, symmetry, proximity, continuity, simplicity, balance, closure, and stability.
It has a high redundancy of visual elements, many of which can be eliminated without loss of recognition but with a severe loss of the aesthetic experience.

means that there is little uncertainty in the probability that the symbols will be identified, even when some of the redundant information is missing. *The experience itself, however, would be different.*

The Gestalt laws operate to reduce uncertainty by facilitating the grouping of visual elements—by redundancy of information. Information that is easily grouped is said to have properties for Prägnanz (Gestalt theory) or redundancy (Information theory). Roughly speaking then, the Gestalt laws of perceptual organization describe various types of redundancy. The Gestalt laws are easy to comprehend but are not easily quantifiable. Information theory, although quantifiable, is more difficult to grasp and leads to error when one tries to use it to quantify human perception.

A Bit of Philosophy

This thou must always bear in mind, what is the nature of the whole, and what is thy nature, and how this is related to that, and what kind of a part it is of what kind of a whole; and that there is no one who hinders thee from always doing and saying the things which are according to the nature of which thou art a part.
—MARCUS AURELIUS

6. Summary

SUMMARY

Verbal

Photographic

Graphic

GESTALT LAWS

Proximity

Similarity

Continuity

Closure

Figure 69.

Verbal Summary

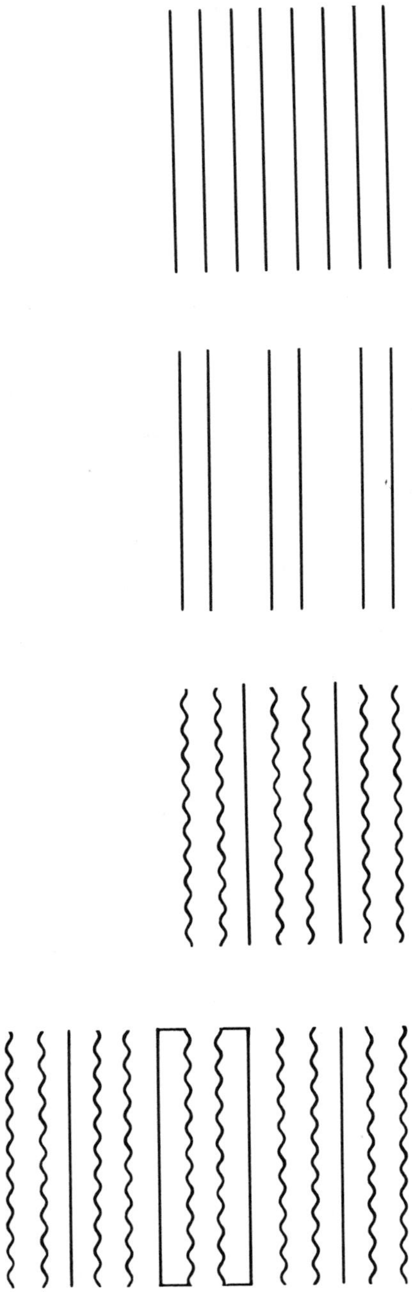

Figure 70.

A. Visual elements that are
similar and an equal distance
apart are very difficult to group.

B. PROXIMITY.
Visual elements that are in close
proximity are readily grouped
together and seen as figure.

C. SIMILARITY.
Visual elements an equal
distance apart are readily
grouped according to their
similarity and seen as figure.

D. SIMILARITY AND CLOSURE.
Dissimilar visual elements at
equal distances are readily
grouped if their area is closed.

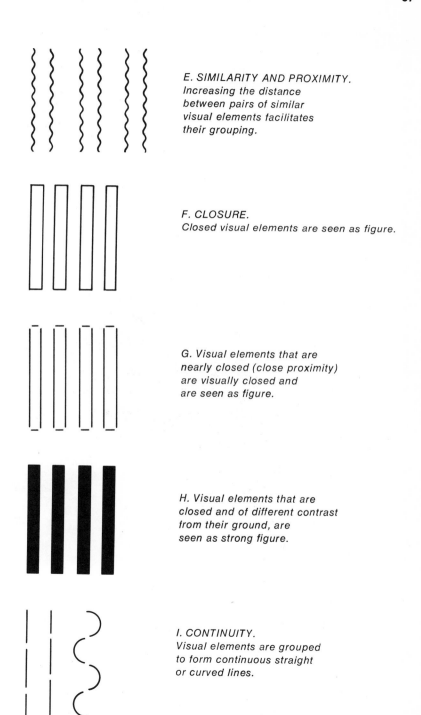

E. SIMILARITY AND PROXIMITY.
Increasing the distance
between pairs of similar
visual elements facilitates
their grouping.

F. CLOSURE.
Closed visual elements are seen as figure.

G. Visual elements that are
nearly closed (close proximity)
are visually closed and
are seen as figure.

H. Visual elements that are
closed and of different contrast
from their ground, are
seen as strong figure.

I. CONTINUITY.
Visual elements are grouped
to form continuous straight
or curved lines.

**Photographic
Summary**

The grouping of visual elements is facilitated if they:

a) are distinct from their background (figure-ground);
b) are close to each other (proximity);
c) are similar in shape, color, texture, size, etc. (similarity);
d) have the fewest interruptions (continuation);
e) allow for formation of something (closure).

Figure 71. BALLOONS by John J. Dowdell III

FIGURE-GROUND   Casper the Ghost? The eye of Casper becomes something else when ground is seen as figure.

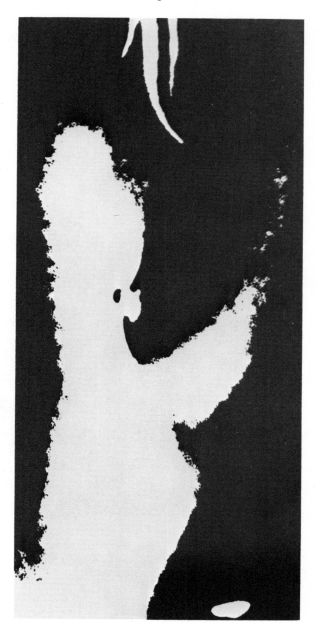

Figure 72.   by Barry Myers

PROXIMITY   Because of their similarity in shape the three sandstone monuments form a group. The farthest two, however, group as a pair because of their similarity in size and shape and also their closeness to each other. The space between the sandstones as well as the cast shadows provide some interesting patterns.

Figure 73.   ERODED SANDSTONES, Monument Park, Colorado by William H. Jackson *(Courtesy George Eastman House)*

SIMILARITY   Married couples grow more alike as their marriage matures. Notice how tenderly Bresson has revealed this through the similarity of facial expressions, hand expressions, and the similarity of dress.

Figure 74.   IRENE AND FREDERIC JOLIOT-CURIE, 1945 by Henri Cartier Bresson

PROXIMITY AND SIMILARITY

Figure 75. ATHENS, 1953 by Henri Cartier Bresson

SYMMETRY

Figure 76.   by Jerry Uelsmann

CONTINUATION The photographer has designed these pairs of photographs so that there is a continuation of line which serves to group them. (These photographs also illustrate why the alignment of projected multiple images is so critical.)

Figure 77. by Mark Wollwage

CLOSURE When you are told that this is an action photograph of a tennis player, the white area is seen more clearly as the figure of a man swinging and hitting a tennis ball. The oval black area at the top of the picture becomes closed when it is seen as the top of the man's head. (Some people have seen the white area in the upper right as the profile of a white eagle.)

Figure 78. TENNIS by Andrew Davidhazy

CONTINUATION AND CLOSURE

Tripping the camera shutter at the instant when the man was positioned as he is provides for a continuity and closure of the half circles. The specular reflection from the man's monocle outlines the circular shape of the glass, which complements the nearly complete large circular shapes.

Figure 79. VALENCIA 1933 by Henri Cartier Bresson

**GESTALT
IDENTIFICATION**

Identify the Gestalt laws operating in the photographs that follow.

by A. Brigman

(Courtesy George
Eastman House)

Figure 80.

MAN IN BOAT
by P. H. Emerson

(Courtesy George
Eastman House)

Figure 81.

SALT LAKE COUNTY, UTAH, 1872 by W. H. Jackson

Figure 82. Quarrying granite in Cottonwood Canyon, to be used for the Mormon Tabernacle. Notice how the workers are grouped. (Courtesy U.S. Dept. of Interior, Denver, Colorado)

TYPES D'ANNAMITES (From LE TONKIN)

Figure 83. (Courtesy George Eastman House)

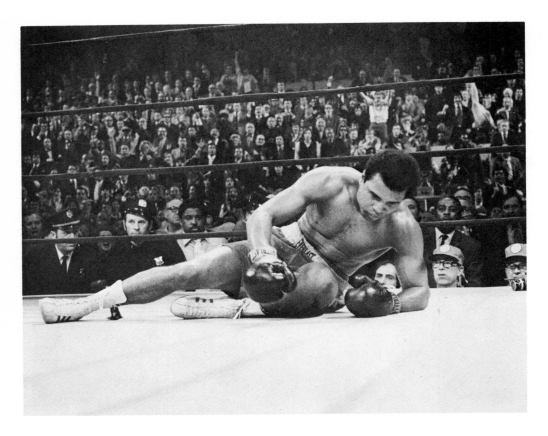

Figure 84. BOXER *(Courtesy New York Daily News)*

Figure 85.

SMILES?
by Abby Perlmutter

Figure 86. SCENIC by George DeWolfe

Figure 87. SOLDIERS by John J. Dowdell III

Figure 88. CHILDREN by John J. Dowdell III

Figure 89. REACHING OUT by John Massey

Figure 90. by Neal Barr *(Courtesy Vanity Fair)*

Figure 91. ROCK AND SHADOW by R. Schottenfeld

Figure 92. by Jonathan B. Atkin

Figure 93. MARCEL MARCEAU by Jonathan B. Atkin

*Graphic
Summary*

Figure 94. Designed by Harvey Carapella

GRAPHICS　　The designs of many of the international graphic symbols presently in use and being proposed provide excellent examples of the Gestalt laws. The few shown here were selected from the several thousand categorized by H. Dreyfuss.* Two religious symbols, the Star of David and that for Yin-Yang, remind us that graphic symbols go far back into history and that their design is ageless.

Figure 95. Star of David

GESTALT

The graphic symbol for Judaism is seen as a total configuration of a star, not as six separate triangles surrounding a hexagon. *The whole is different from the sum of its parts.*

Figure 96. Yin Yang

FIGURE-GROUND

The graphic symbol for Taoism, representing Yin Yang, is perfectly symmetrical, either half being seen as figure or ground.

Figure 97. Rotate, Clockwise

PROXIMITY

The closeness of the small bars allows easy grouping into a clockwise movement.

---

*H. Dreyfuss and R. Fuller, *Symbol Sourcebook* (New York: McGraw-Hill Book Co., 1972).

SIMILARITY

Figure 98.
A. Bright or hazy sun; sand; snow.
B. Cloudy bright, no shadows.

A   B

The wavy lines are similar and, therefore, are grouped together. A special case of similarity is *symmetry.* All the visual elements in the picture are balanced. Cut either picture through the center and each half contains the same image.

SYMMETRY

Figure 99.
A. Water sports area.
B. Shooting.

A   B

CONTINUATION

Figure 100. Chaff.

The wavy line is easier seen as one continuous line than not.

CLOSURE

Figure 101. Radioactive.

The three dark segments are easily seen since they represent closed segments. The similar unenclosed (white) segments are extremely difficult to see.

SIMILARITY
PROXIMITY
CONTINUATION
CLOSURE

Figure 102.
A. Ice hockey.
B. Cross-country skiing.

A   *B*

All four Gestalt laws are readily identified in these olympic graphics. The dark wavy lines are *similar* in contour, but vary in thickness. The closed dark wavy lines are narrower than the white lines and are, therefore, more readily seen as figure. In certain areas the dark wavy lines become thicker (greater *proximity*) and facilitate a grouping of visual elements in that area. The dark wavy lines that vary in thickness and therefore proximity facilitate a *continuation* of line at the very edges where the thickness of the dark lines changes.

Similarity, proximity, and continuation work together to facilitate the *closure* of a person in action. This closure provides meaning and psychological balance (Prägnanz).

7. Gestalt Exercises

A description of how this photograph was made appears in the appendix.

Candy Bars

What is contained in the background influences the foreground. In the example below the Hershey Park sign has a circular top and a curved lower section that is concave and similar to the top. Photographing such a sign from the wrong position can introduce a background that interferes with this harmony of shape.

Photograph similar situations yourself so that the background of a picture becomes as obvious to you as the foreground. Try different ways of controlling the background. Change of camera position is one, selective focus, another.

ATTENTION TO BACKGROUND   NO ATTENTION TO BACKGROUND

Arrows   Take two or more visual elements that are similar, such as the arrows below, and arrange them to form interesting and symmetrical patterns.

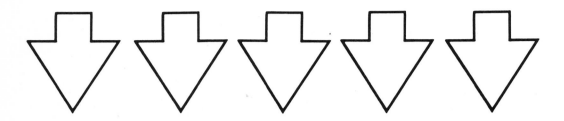

I have used four arrows to make the arrangement below. Notice how the Gestalt laws of similarity, proximity, continuity, and closure are operating to facilitate a grouping of the visual elements —to facilitate a good Gestalt. Note also the figure-ground relationship.

Profiles   Examine the importance of symmetry and proximity in figure-
ground relationships by arranging picture situations in which
there is perfect symmetry, varying degrees of dissymmetry, and
varying distances between two figures. Study the effect of closed
areas on figure-ground by retracing these profiles so that the
center area is closed, but not the profiles.

SYMMETRICAL

ASYMMETRICAL

PROXIMITY

Look Around   Take your camera and look for things in nature that you can photograph to illustrate figure-ground, proximity, similarity, continuity, and closure. Look also for man-made objects, such as sculp-
ture, architecture, signs, and the like, that possess these Gestalt
characteristics. All you have to do is to train yourself to see them.
What you will be doing for the most part is discovering what
someone else has designed. This is a valid way of learning.
Artists and craftsman have copied the works of masters as a way
of developing visual-tactile skills. The more difficult task, perhaps,
is to discover objects or arrangement of objects that will group
together according to the Gestalt laws. Look through photographic books such as *The World of Henri Cartier Bresson** with
the Gestalt laws in mind.

*See References.

by George Weidert

All Stars

Designs from nature are often incorporated in things man designs. The number of stars in the vice-presidential flag is 13; in the presidential flag, 50 (Fig. 56A and B). This seems to be based on the number of original colonies and the present number of states. If this were not a consideration, what is the fewest number of stars necessary to form a circle?

Trace or copy the vice-presidential flag shown in Fig. 56A. Try adding just the right number of stars to form closure of a circle. What is the minimum number required? Try the reverse with the presidential flag.

For variation try adding to the vice-presidential flag visual elements other than stars to form a circle.

Return to the General of the Army flag (Fig. 55). Trace the pentagon shape in the center of the flag and note how easy it is to make a star of it. Do the opposite with any one of the five stars. Again trace the pentagon shape, but this time trace one of the stars so that it is centered within the pentagon. Now vary the area of the star within the pentagon and discover the many interesting figure-ground relationships you can generate. Try variations such as open-closed areas, rotation of the pentagon shape, and shading.

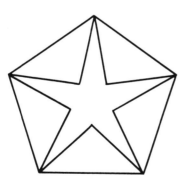

STAR WITHIN A PENTAGON AND VARIATION

Paper Clips   Take a few ordinary paper clips and open them up to form the shape below. Then try various arrangements to illustrate grouping.

PAPER CLIP OPENED   ARRANGED FOR GROUPING

Try opening the paper clip to different shapes and arrange for various groupings.

DIFFERENT SHAPE   ONE POSSIBLE ARRANGEMENT

If you have access to an overhead projector you can use it to enlarge the arrangements you make. You can do the same thing, of course, with an enlarger. If you want a record of your arrangement, make a print or simply arrange the opened clips on photographic paper and make photograms.

If you do not have ready access to equipment and want to make a record of the arrangements, start out by tracing the shape of the single opened paper clip on paper. Then use tracing paper to trace out various arrangements.

As you develop the various groupings identify the Gestalt laws that are facilitating the groupings.

Typography Search out different styles of typeface being used in advertising and identify the Gestalt laws that are operating. Try styling your own type. Check your library for books on typography.

MIND

UNITED STATES

**Light
a Candle**

As far back as the early days of Rome there are examples of artists grouping letters in such a way as to form shapes of objects.* Use different styles of type and arrange them to form familiar objects. Modify existing styles or design your own if necessary.

*Many fine examples of this and novel letter forms can be found in *Letter and Image* by Massin (New York: Van Nostrand Reinhold Co., 1970).

Dot's Nice

Look at photographs that are reproduced in newspapers and magazines through a magnifying glass. You will notice dots of different darkness, size, and shape. You no longer see them as a picture because you have magnified the distance between the dots (visual elements).

In the grid below darken the dotted squares and then back off until the proximity between the visual elements facilitates grouping so that you see a picture. Try making one up for others.

(In the appendix on p. 152 you will find a completed grid of the same picture but with five different gray values. Compare it to the grid you have filled in using only two values, white and black.)

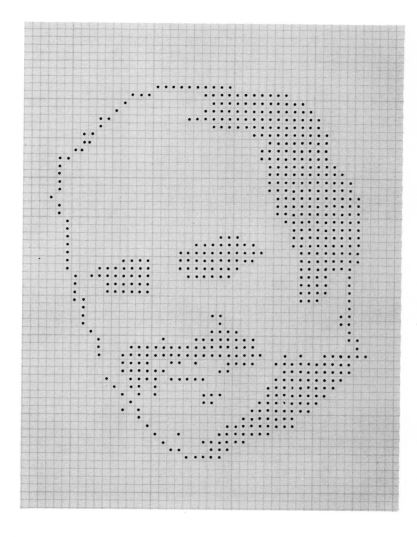

More Dots

How far back do you have to get before all the dots group together and blend? Such a technique is used as one way to estimate the graininess of a photograph. The farther back you have to go before a photograph is no longer seen as grainy, the higher the graininess. All photographs are grainy. If you do not believe it just look at one through a magnifying glass or microscope.

by Larry McKnight

Computer-Generated "Dots"

There are contained 225 small squares of discrete lightnesses (values) within the upper left square. Each little square is the same size. As you proceed from left to right and downward the small squares get progressively smaller and their number increases, but the discrete range of lightnesses remains the same. Resolution increases and the picture of the eye becomes more distinguishable. *The whole is different from the sum of its parts.* (Resolution can be increased for the less distinguishable pictures by increasing the viewing distance.)

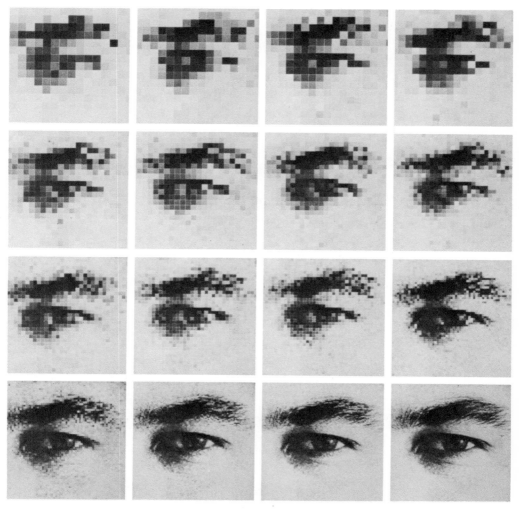

A snapshot of the human eye was digitized on a programmable film reader (PFR) by Information International, Los Angeles, to convert it from visual to electronic stimuli. The data was processed with a special picture program and then rerecorded in a mosaic sequence of increasing resolution. (Courtesy Society of Photographic Scientists and Engineers)

Scrap Book Start a scrap book of various examples of the Gestalt laws that you can identify in magazines. Cut out pictures and illustrations and paste them in your scrapbook with proper identification. You may want to lay out your book in a way similar to this one with examples of:

a) figure-ground;
b) proximity;
c) similarity;
d) continuity;
e) closure; and
f) Prägnanz.

An easy way to start is by collecting graphic identity marks of different organizations. You could also include some of your own photographs or even take photographs especially for this purpose. Do it with a friend and compare your scrapbooks.

Designer: Fiberboard Paper Products

Designer: Bruce Montgomery

Designer: Charles Coiner

Designer: Saul Bass

Save Stamps

Start looking for stamps that have incorporated in their design some of the Gestalt laws of perceptual organization. You will be surprised at how many you can find once you begin looking for them. Do not limit yourself to any one country. Stop at a stamp collector's store and look around. Start a collection.

*More
Stamps*

TV Screen

Consider your TV screen as a source of moving and changing pictures in which each "frame" is on for 1/30th of a second. In one second's time you have an opportunity to photograph thirty different pictures; in one minute, up to 1800 different pictures.

Place your camera so that you can focus on the entire TV screen and set the shutter speed at 1/30th of a second.* If you are using a film with an ASA speed of 160 (DIN 23) set the aperture at about f/2.8.

Sit close to your camera with your finger on the shutter release. Think of one of the Gestalt laws and watch the changing TV pictures until you see an image that has a Gestalt design. Quickly take a photograph of it.

Shoot off a few rolls of film this way and then study the results. It is an excellent way to develop your perception and timing so that you can capture pictures that exist for only a fleeting second.

*If your camera has a focal-plane shutter use a shutter speed of 1/10th of a second. For additional information and helpful hints write to the Consumer Market Division, Eastman Kodak Co., Rochester, New York, 14650 and ask for a copy of *Photography of Television Images.*

PICTURES FROM A TV SCREEN

**Cloud
Watching**

Cloud watching has been a favorite pastime of children through-out the ages. They look at the clouds as they move through the sky, grouping together, separating and changing brightnesses. Watch them for awhile armed with a camera and when you see an interesting figure-ground, photograph it. If you are using black-and-white film try a yellow or a red filter. For color film use a polarizing filter.

In the early 1900s Alfred Stieglitz produced hundreds of pho-tographs of clouds which he called "equivalents." The feelings evoked by looking at such images were, for him, equivalent to similar feelings he had experienced by other means.

Such experiences are related to the Gestalt concept of *isomorphism* which implies equality of form. Koffka has a lengthy discussion of this in his book *Principles of Gestalt Psychology.*

CLOUDS by Mark Wollwage

"Ground"
Watching

Look for interesting "ground" in clouds, trees and shadows. The picture below becomes interesting when you group "figure" with the shadow it casts. The photograph is also of interest in terms of the symbolism you might care to read into it.

Look up at the branches and leaves of a tree against a sky background. Consider the space between the leaves as figure and scan slowly until you see an interesting pattern. Photograph it and study it later. Try exposing the film at two different levels of exposure. Expose for detail in the leaves and then stop down and expose for the sky. Try the same procedure for the shadows of the leaves on the ground.

If you have a single reflex camera or equivalent, look through it as you scan the leaves of the tree. Your perceptions will be different.

FIGURE
AND GROUND
AS FIGURE

Camouflage   Practice the art of camouflage by taking a common object such as a pencil, scissors, film can, coin, ball, cigar, pipe, or book and arrange it along with other objects so that it is very difficult to distinguish. The directions for doing this are simple—apply the Gestalt laws. Doing it is difficult, but the difficulty decreases with practice.

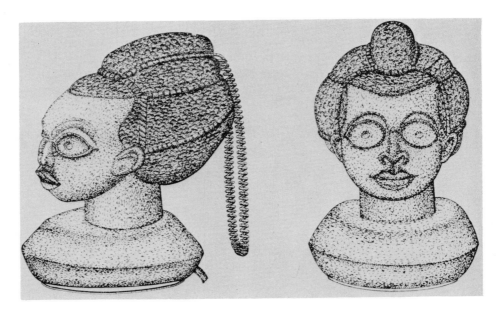

FIND THE TELEPHONE
(U.S. Design Patent 225,413 by Allen W. Scoggins)

Symmetry

Some photographs can be made more interesting simply by repeating certain parts of the picture. This can be done using techniques such as double exposures, combination printing, and paste-ups. This commercial illustration is given added interest by the symmetrical juxtaposition of key elements. Note also how the offsetting of the vertical shaft gives variety to something that might otherwise look too orderly.

Mentally play around with ways of cropping this photograph to get other designs. Remember the importance of area and contrast, of closure, and so on.

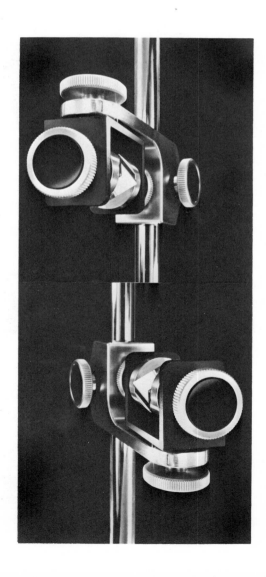

Photographic
Jigsaw

Take some of your old photographs or those printed in magazines and cut them up into smaller pieces. Lay them out on a table as you would a jigsaw puzzle. Now select pieces and arrange them in a way so that they will group.

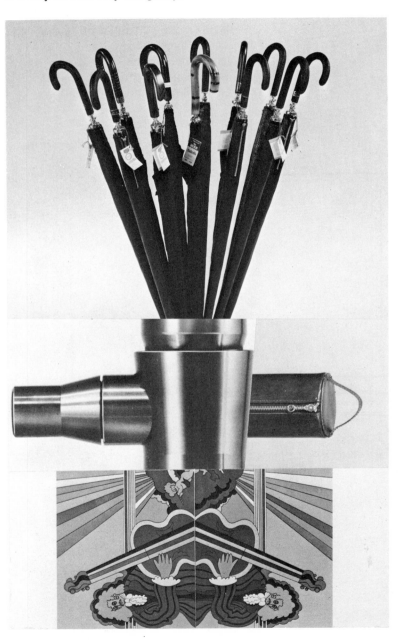

Page
Layout

The Gestalt laws of organization can be found in good page layout, whether in magazines or yearbooks. Items that are to be grouped together will be in close proximity and similar in some sense. There will be continuity of line and opportunities for closure. You can also find symmetry and order, but there will be variations to prevent the page layout from becoming static. For good examples of layout look at the better magazines and yearbooks; for poor examples look at almost any newspaper. A good way to lay out visual components such as photographs, typography, and illustrations is to use some kind of grid, for example, graph paper. Try a symmetrical layout. Remember that the spaces (ground) between the visual components (figure) are very important as is the content of the pictures (lines, shape, texture, etc.)

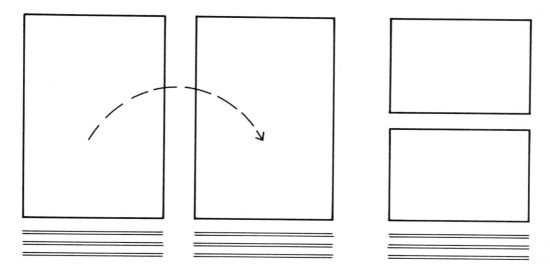

Page layout showing proximity, similarity, symmetry,
and continuation of frame line and content line.

**Flower
Arranging**

The Gestalt laws of perceptual organization can be used in arranging flowers so that they are seen as being grouped together; the whole organization of flowers is different from any one flower.

SIMILARITY

Select flowers that are similar in shape, size, color or texture and place them in *proximity* to each other so that you can readily group them as you plan. If you arrange them so that they can be seen as a *continuation* of visual elements that make up a familiar form, such as a triangle, half circle, etc., *closure* will occur, and the person looking at the floral arrangement will in effect be looking at a live "picture" you have created.

Contrast can be added by including visual elements that are not similar in shape, size, and color, such as leaves, pussy willows, etc. Remember that the space between the visual elements (flowers and other objects) is ground and plays an important role in the perception of figure. While arranging the floral elements into a total picture remember that a good Gestalt is one that allows for easy grouping of all the visual elements into an organized whole and that this organized whole has a visual feeling of balance or equilibrium (Prägnanz).

***Cropping
and Mounting***

The Gestalt laws can help you while you are framing a picture in a camera viewfinder or cropping a picture that is being printed. Notice in the photograph below how careful the photographer was in framing the scene. She wanted to show the similarity of shapes between natural terrain and animals. Her tight framing of the upper section of the white and black horses does this dramatically.

She was also mindful of the white area on which her photograph was to be mounted so that the lower black area is closed by the white mountboard, and the white area is closed by the dark area of the photograph itself.

by Liza Jones

8. Gestalt Games

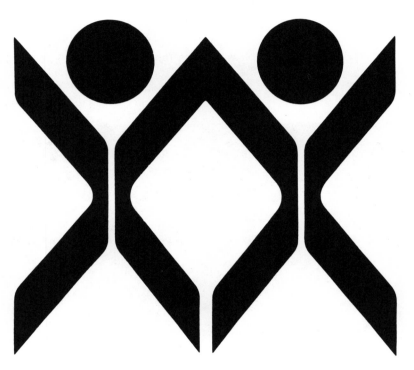

Design by Latham Tyler and Sherman Mutchnick

***Photo
Rorschach***

In psychological testing a Rorschach Inkblot Test is sometimes used. The ink blot is easily made by dropping some ink on a piece of white paper and then folding it across the middle. What results is a bilaterally symmetrical "image." Persons are asked to look at it and tell what they see. A trained psychologist works with a standardized set of such images and, from previous information, knows what the most probable responses will be when a person is asked to tell what he sees.

Instead of using ink and paper, use developer and photograph paper and make your own symmetrical images. Here is how.

1. Expose a thin sheet of 5×7 paper.
2. Fold it.
3. Drop some developer into the fold.
4. Refold and let develop.
5. Open and fix.

Some of the responses people gave when they looked at the photo Rorschach shown here were: butterfly, two insects climbing a pole, x-ray of a pelvis and violin. What does it look like to you?

PHOTO RORSCHACH
by Barry Myers

What do you see?

Verbal Figure-Ground

When you first look at the 9×10 letter matrix below you see an array of letters. When you are told, however, that these letters make up words and that the words run in various directions—horizontal, vertical and diagonal—you begin to separate figure from ground. Try it. Look for these words and draw a line around them when you find them. (Please note: some letters are common to more than one word.)

ASA
APERTURE
CAMERA
COLOR
DEVELOP
EXPOSURE
FILM
FILTER
FOCUS
GESTALT
HYPO
LENS
PHOTO
SHUTTER
TRIPOD

```
D A P O L E V E D E
O S R C A M E R A R
P A P E R T U R E U
I R H R E T T U H S
R O O C O L O R N O
T P T F R T N E B P
L Y O R E T L I F X
T H G E S T A L T E
M L I F O C U S R T
```

Words   Make up a matrix of four words shown below and then ask a person to read the words you have written. Time how long it takes. How many four-letter words? Do you see any other words?

```
T E A R
H O P E
E V E N
N O O N
```

Now have him try the word matrices below. The horizontal words are, of course, obvious. Reflect on how you searched for the other words by scanning for letters (visual elements) that you could *group* together meaningfully.

```
T I R E      M A S H      O R A L
S H I N      E C H O      M A R E
N I C E      C O O L      E V E N
P E E K      C A P S      N E A T
```

What do you notice about these matrices?

```
K I N G      G N A T      A N N A
I D E A      N O V A      N O O N
N E X T      A V O N      N O O N
G A T E      T A N G      A N N A
```

What relationship do you notice between these matrices?

```
R A T      F I R S T
A C E      I R A T E
T E A      R A C E R
         S T E A M
         T E R M S
```

If you enjoy word games of this kind, pick up the paperback *Language on Vacation: An Olio of Orthographical Oddities* by Dmitri A. Borgmann (New York: Charles Scribner's Sons, 1965).

**Canadian
Capers**

The present Canadian flag was officially adopted in 1965. The center of the flag contains the profile of a red maple leaf. It also contains the profiles of two men that appear to be ramming heads in much the same manner that elk do. Look closely in the upper right- and left-hand sides of the maple leaf. Both men have a common forehead.

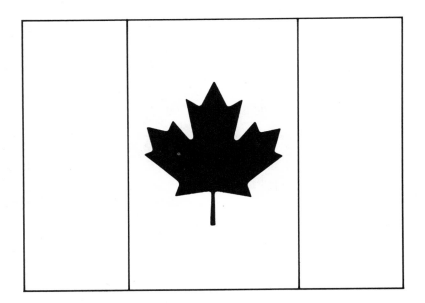

Amen   Symmetrical repetition of the same visual elements provides interesting patterns. Try some.

by Roger Remington

***Same
or Different***

Are the two illustrations below similar? It will probably take you a little while looking and thinking to decide. (The answer is at the bottom of the page.)

After you have answered the question and looked at the answer, look again at the images and see if you can find the Star of David. Look for other groupings.

ANSWER: They are exactly the same except for orientation. It is more difficult to see subtle difference than gross difference. One might also question the question: Similar in what respects?

Closure

Look through magazines and newspapers and cut out pictures of various familiar objects. Then trace them, leaving out sections of the line tracing. Ask your friends to identify the objects. You can increase the interest by timing how long it takes each person to identify each object. It is also of interest to find out how incomplete a tracing can be and still allow identification (closure).

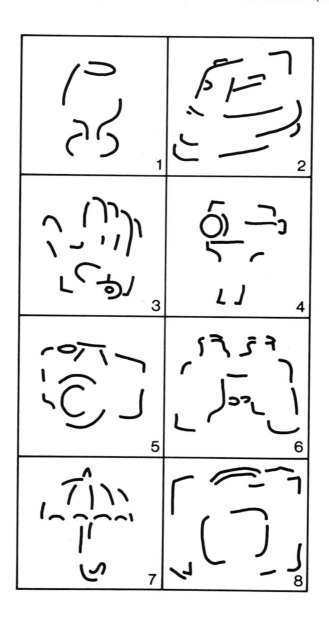

Visual
Elements

Place a piece of tracing paper over a picture of some object and trace out a series of small lines that can later be grouped and used to identify the object. Do several of these and have a friend identify the objects. The challenge is to use the fewest number of visual elements and still provide for quick identification. You will find the Gestalt laws of proximity, similarity, continuation, and closure very much in evidence as you do this.

The fact that you can construct a picture from such limited information indicates the amount of redundancy in any picture. This is why artists can sketch the essentials of a picture with a minimum of lines. In terms of information theory, the essential information or uncertainty is concentrated in regions where there are abrupt changes. It is only when a straight or curved line changes direction that redundancy is lost and uncertainty begins.

How long did it take you to group these visual elements and form closure?

**Greasy
Graphics**

Some very interesting images can be made by using a little grease and photographic paper. In the illustration below John Dowdell coated his face with a thin film of petroleum jelly. He then carefully pressed his face against the emulsion side of a sheet of photographic paper, making sure not to smear the jelly. When the paper is developed, areas that have been touched by the jelly remain white and the rest of the area darkens. The technique is as follows: after development run the paper through water or a stop bath and fix for a few minutes. Then wipe off the jelly with a paper towel, fix for a few more minutes, wash, and dry.

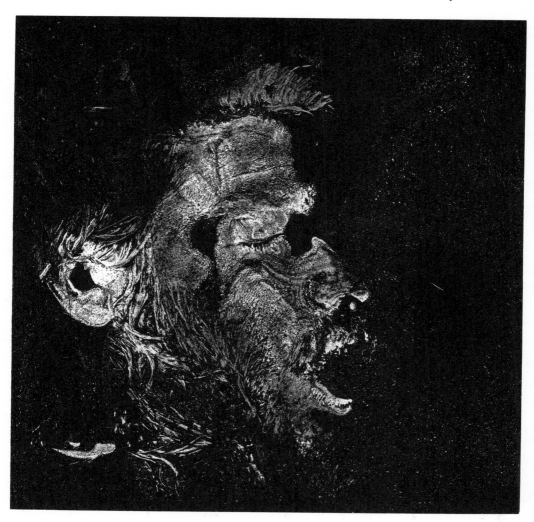

by John J. Dowdell III

Hide and Seek The Gestalt laws facilitate the grouping of visual elements to provide Prägnanz. They can also be used to hide or imbed good figures. For example, you would hardly expect to find the nuclear disarmament symbol or the letter Z in the arrangements below.

HIDE   SEEK   HIDE   SEEK

Both figures are lost because the visual system has incorporated them into a different and more easily seen pattern. *The whole is different from the sum of its parts.* The law of good continuation is operating to facilitate grouping according to the least number of interruptions or changes of line.

Here are some figures for you to hide and have someone seek.

  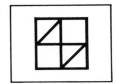

Seek the hidden familiar figures.

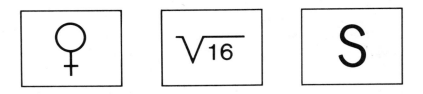

Find the Star   Look at the illustration below and see if you can form a closure on a star within the large star. Similarity of shapes, proximity of shapes, and continuity of line make it very difficult.

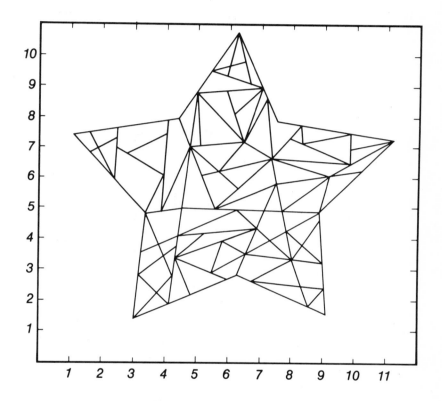

ANSWER: You can find the center of the star at coordinates $x = 7.2$, $y = 4.5$. Did you, however, happen to see the forest in spite of the trees—i.e., the large star?

Tangrams A tangram is a seven-piece Chinese puzzle similar to our jigsaw puzzle in that the object of the game is to fit pieces together. It is quite different from a jigsaw puzzle, however, since it contains only seven geometric pieces that can be fitted together to form a variety of greater shapes. It is a good example of Gestalt because the figures that result from the various possible combinations of the same seven pieces are different from the sum of the pieces or parts.

The seven pieces that make up a tangram can be traced and cut from the square below:

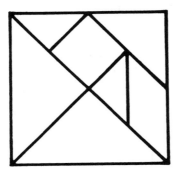

The object of the game is to group these seven pieces to form figures other than squares, such as a cat.

 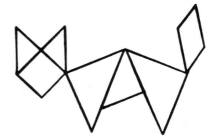

The task is difficult because there are many different ways in which the seven pieces can be positioned, and mentally, visually, and with your fingers you must group them to make a whole figure.

Note that even when the seven parts are clearly shown the initial tendency is not to see seven individual parts but to see the totality of these parts grouped into the form of a cat. Here are some for you to try. (The answers are in the Appendix.)

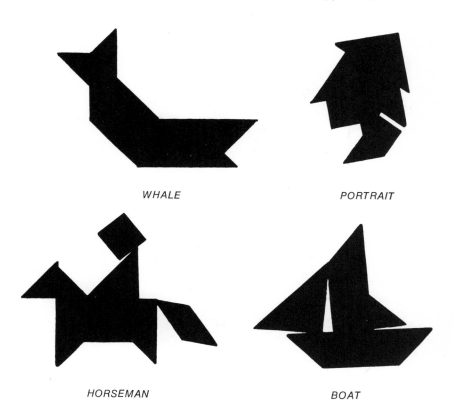

WHALE   PORTRAIT

HORSEMAN   BOAT

If you are interested in more of these tangrams, pick up a copy of the paperback book *Tangrams, 330 Puzzles.** The cost is about $2.00.

*Ronald C. Read, *Tangrams, 330 Puzzles* (New York: Dover Publications, 1965).

**Don't Be a
Square**

Try solving this visual-tactile problem if you have not seen it before. If you have seen it, try it on a friend and observe how he
attempts to solve it.

Given the array of nine dots below, connect them all together
with only four straight lines. You are not allowed to lift your pencil
from the paper. Try solving the 16-dot problem using the same
technique. (The answers appear in the Appendix.)

9 Dots—Connect the dots with four straight lines.

16 Dots—Connect the dots with only six straight lines.

Appendix

Dalmatian
Figure-Ground

The original negative of the Dalmatian dog (see Figure 13) was made on Tri-X film using a 35mm camera. The film was exposed and developed in a normal manner. The negative was then printed onto an 8 × 10 high-contrast grade paper to eliminate some of the intermediate tones between white and black. This print was then photographed onto direct-positive line photostat using the Kodak PMT system. This photostat was retouched by hand, removing leash and other extraneous imagery. Final print was another PMT Photostat.

Gestalt
Exercises
Illustration

A detailed description of how to obtain line effects from photographs can be found in the free Kodak booklet *Tone-Line Process* (Eastman Kodak Company, 343 State Street, Rochester, New York 14650, Dept. 454).

Briefly, this is how the process works:

1. Contact print a negative image onto a film material to produce a positive image.
2. Superimpose the negative and positive image back to back and tape them at the edges. (You will notice that when you do this, all you can see are the boundaries of the images. All other tones cancel out.)
3. Make a contact print from the combined negative and positive sandwich onto a high-contrast material such as Kodalith Ortho Film.

**Dot's Nice
(Four Tones)**

Screened photograph using only two values and four different
values from white to black.

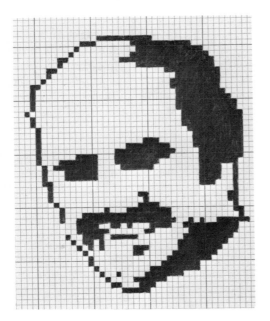

TWO VALUES (WHITE AND BLACK)

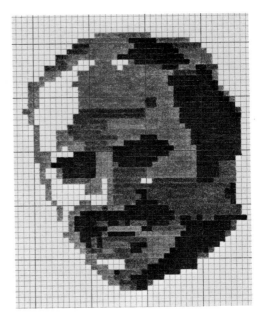

*FOUR VALUES (WHITE, LIGHT GRAY,
DARK GRAY, AND BLACK)*

**Answers to
Tangrams**

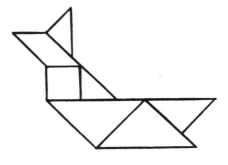

WHALE

PORTRAIT

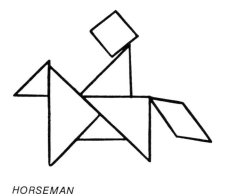

HORSEMAN

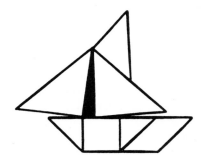

BOAT

Answers to the Visual-Tactile Puzzles

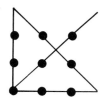

9-DOT PUZZLE

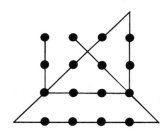

16-DOT PUZZLE

An important perceptual lesson can be learned from these simple puzzles. Do not impose limitations or constraints upon yourself. Force yourself to organize things differently—to see things differently. Most people will see the nine-dot array as forming a square; this is predictable, based on the Gestalt laws of similarity, proximity, continuity, and closure. Unconsciously then, one assumes the problem must be solved within the confines of that imaginary square. The moment this position is accepted, the solver has imprisoned himself, and the problem is not solvable. A good photographer will force himself to think and see differently, and by doing so will produce new and exciting pictures. Look around at pictures you find exciting and creative and notice if the photographer isn't seeing things in a new fashion.

References

The selected references that follow will provide you with an opportunity to go deeper into the Gestalt approach to perception and to expand into related areas, including the new area of the study of perception called *information processing.* Brief descriptions are given for each reference to guide and encourage you to go further into the study of visual perception.

For convenience the references are divided into three sections: inexpensive paperbacks, hardbacks, and *Scientific American* articles.

PAPERBACKS

Arnheim, R., *Art and Visual Perception.*
Berkeley, Calif.: University of California Press, 1969.

Dr. Arnheim has spent a lifetime relating Gestalt psychology to art. This comprehensive book, first published in 1954, is very useful to the inquiry and understanding of why we see what we see in art. A word of caution, however; in the past 20 years new knowledge regarding perception requires modification of some of the generalizations made in the book.

Arnheim, R., *Entropy and Art.*
Berkeley, Calif.: University of California Press, 1971.

A treatise that attempts to clarify the confusion that results when the language and concepts of information theory are used rigidly to explain art.

Arnheim, R., *Toward A Psychology of Art.*
Berkeley, Calif.: University of California Press, 1972.

A collection of papers written over a twenty-five-year period based on the assumption that art, as any other activity of the mind, is subject to psychology, accessible to understanding, and needed for any comprehensive survey of mental functioning. This book is a continuation of Art and Visual Perception *and addresses itself to those teaching art as well as to those practicing it.*

Arnheim, R., *Visual Thinking.*
Berkeley, Calif.: University of California Press, 1972.

A convincing argument that artistic activities such as painting, photographing, designing, composing, etc., are forms of reasoning and thinking in which perceiving and thinking are indivisibly related. Arnheim's posit that there is an orchestration of all the senses and thinking during artistic activities reflects his Gestalt approach to understanding human perception.

Giannetti, L. D., *Understanding Movies.*
Englewood Cliffs, N.J.: Prentice-Hall, Inc., 1972.

A very well-written, profusely-illustrated book that tells and shows the basic techniques used by film directors in organizing sight and sound elements so they convey meaning and feeling. Chapters cover the picture, movement, editing, sound, drama, literature, and theory. The book relates well to the Gestalt laws of organization.

Gombrich, E. H., *Art and Illusion.*
Princeton, N.J.: Princeton University Press, 1969.

Professor Gombrich concerns himself with theories of visual perception, information, and learning as they give new insights into the history and psychology of pictorial representation. An excellent and well-illustrated book for learning the techniques of representation used by early artists.

Gregory, R. L., *Eye and Brain.*
New York: McGraw-Hill, 1966.

This is a book about the psychology of seeing. It is easy to read with excellent illustrations on nearly every page. A good book to start with for those interested in an introduction to visual perception.

Hochberg, J. E., *Perception.*
Englewood Cliffs, N.J.: Prentice-Hall, Inc., 1964.

Although it is just 118 pages, this book is jampacked with information on perception and is very well illustrated. Each chapter has a summary and there is an excellent section on the Gestalt laws. A good book for those who want to go further into the general area of perception.

Hornung, G. P., *Handbook of Design and Devices.*
New York: Dover Publications, Inc., 1959.

A compilation and classification of over 1800 basic geometric designs for quick, convenient reference. This is a fun book to look through and see the applications of the Gestalt laws of organization to graphic design.

Jung, C. G., *Man and His Symbols.*
New York: Dell Publishing Company, 1964.

Dr. Jung wrote this book so that the general reader, with little or no formal background in psychology, could gain an appreciation for the role that dreams and symbols play in man's search for expression and meaning. The book is profusely illustrated with photographs and works of art throughout history. Highly recommended for those who are searching for deeper significance in photographs, art, and design.

Koffka, K., *Principles of Gestalt Psychology.*
New York: Harcourt Brace and World, 1963.

Written by one of the founders of the Gestalt School, this 700-page authoritative book provides a broad, detailed view of the field of Gestalt psychology. There are two chapters of great interest to those who want to learn more about figure-ground relationships and visual organization.

Luckiesh, M., *Visual Illusions.*
New York: Dover Publications, Inc., 1965.

Although this layman's introduction to visual illusions was originally compiled in 1922, it contains illustrations of nearly every known visual illusion. This book is still the best one to begin with if you are interested in learning about visual illusions.

McKim, R. H., *Experiences in Visual Thinking.*
Monterey, Calif.: Brooks Cole, 1972.

Instead of just writing about how we use visual information to think, Mc-Kim provides the reader with an opportunity to think visually by solving hundreds of visual problems. An excellent complement to Arnheim's Visual Thinking.

Tolansky, S., *Optical Illusions.*
Elmsford, N.Y.: Pergamon Press, 1964.

Written for the layman by a physicist to call attention to how human judgments of physical qualities can be erroneous because of visual illusions. Well-illustrated.

Zakia, R. D., and H. N. Todd, *101 Experiments in Photography.*
Dobbs Ferry, New York: Morgan and Morgan, 1973.

This book was designed to expand a person's interest in photography by suggesting a variety of simple experiments. Of special interest are twelve experiments in vision and illusions.

HARDBACKS

The Art of Photography.
New York: Time Inc., 1971.

One of a series of Time-Life books on Photography. There are many excellent photographs and an easy-to-read text that is characteristic of the entire series. You will find the section on "Principles of Design" especially interesting.

Bresson, H. C., *The World of Henri Cartier Bresson.*
New York: Viking Press, 1968.

A book of photographs by a photographer who believes that " . . . composition should be a constant preoccupation, being a simultaneous coalition, an organic coordination of visual elements." You will be able to identify the Gestalt laws in many of Bresson's photographs.

Carraker, R. G., and J. B. Thurston, *Optical Illusions and the Visual Arts.*
New York: Van Nostrand-Reinhold, 1966.

A picture book that shows optical illusions and the part they play in photography, fine art, and graphic art. Contains a comprehensive glossary of optical illusions.

Dondis, D., *A Primer of Visual Literacy.*
Cambridge, Mass.: The MIT Press, 1973.

An introductory book for anyone interested in the design of visual information. The intent is to teach the interconnected arts of visual communications.

Dreyfuss H., *Symbol Sourcebook.*
New York: McGraw-Hill, 1972.

An authoritative illustrated guide to international graphic symbols by a famous industrial designer, with an introduction by Buckminster Fuller. An excellent source book of visual symbols.

Ellis, W. D., *A Source Book of Gestalt Psychology.*
New York: Humanities Press, 1939.

A scholarly book that translates and summarizes 34 original articles and one book on Gestalt psychology, which were published in Germany between 1915 and 1929. Heavy reading.

Evans, R. M., *Eye, Film, and Camera in Color Photography.*
New York: Wiley, 1960.

Ralph Evans was a photographer and scientist who had spent a lifetime studying color, color photography, and human perception. This unique book brings together perception and photography in a way that is meaningful to a photographer.

Feininger, A., *Photographic Seeing.*
Englewood Cliffs, N.J.: Prentice-Hall, Inc., 1973.

A practical approach to "seeing" as the "camera sees" so that the photographer can take corrective measures when making his photograph.

Forgus, R. H., *Perception.*
New York: McGraw-Hill, 1966.

An excellent textbook on perception, clearly-written and well-illustrated. Many areas of perception are covered, with an especially good section on the Gestalt laws.

Gregory, R. L., *The Intelligent Eye.*
New York: McGraw-Hill, 1970.

An in-depth continuation of Gregory's early book Eye and Brain. *It concerns itself with how the brain function of man has been modified through the invention and use of symbols, especially language and numbers.*

Haber, R. N. and M. Hershenson, *The Psychology of Visual Perception.*
New York: Holt, Rinehart and Winston, 1973.

An authoritative and clearly-written textbook that covers a new area of perception called information processing *(how human beings process information). The more traditional fields of perception, such as the Gestalt laws of organization, are included and related to information processing theory.*

Harlan, C., *Vision and Invention.*
Englewood Cliffs, N.J.: Prentice-Hall, Inc., 1970.

This book is written by an artist-teacher who believes that certain basic principles, pertaining especially to structure, remain remarkably constant regardless of style. Contains many illustrations, references, and experiment-explorations.

Kepes, G., ed., *Module, Proportion, Symmetry, Rhythm.*
New York: George Braziller, 1966.

Authors representing a variety of disciplines explore the role of the basic unit (module) and its combinatory relationships in thinking and creative works. (One of a series of six volumes called Vision and Value.*)*

Key, W. B., *Subliminal Seduction.*
Englewood Cliffs, N.J.: Prentice-Hall, Inc., 1973.

An interesting and provocative book on advertising that reveals how archetypal symbolisms are hidden in pictures so they can appeal to our unconscious. Once these imbedded symbols are seen as figure, the technique for imbedding them also becomes evident.

Kohler, W., *The Task of Gestalt Psychology.*
Princeton, N.J.: Princeton University Press, 1969.

A summary of a series of lectures given at Princeton University by Wolfgang Kohler, one of the founders of Gestalt psychology. This 164-page book is clearly written and serves as an introduction to Gestalt theory.

Millerson, G., *The Technique of Television Production.*
New York: Hastings House, 1970.

Although this is a book about television production, it is more broadly a book about how to design, organize, and produce visual and auditory information. Of particular interest are the sections on picture composition, editing, and aural compositions. The book is so well illustrated, you can learn by just looking at the pictures.

Mueller, C. and M. Rudolph, eds., *Light and Vision.*
New York: Time Inc., 1966.

One of a series of the Life Science Library. Two chapters are of special interest; Three Dimensions of Vision and Seeing with the Brain. A very useful book with many interesting illustrations.

Pastore, N., *Selective History of Theories of Visual Perception: 1650–1950.*
New York: Oxford University Press, 1971.

A well-written history of the theories of perception since the seventeenth century that provides a basis for the appreciation and understanding of our present theories. The author has utilized many of the ideas of Gestalt psychology as expressed by Wertheimer, Kohler, Koffka, and others.

Zusne, L., *Visual Perception of Form.*
New York: Academic Press, 1970.

The most comprehensive survey of what is presently known about form perception, including a section on the Gestalt viewpoint. Heavy reading.

SCIENTIFIC AMERICAN ARTICLES

I have found this select listing of *Scientific American* articles worth reading and studying. Perhaps you will also.

Most of these articles are available as offprints from W. H. Freeman and Company, 660 Market Street, San Francisco, California, 94104.

Attneave, F., *"Multistability in Perception,"* (December, 1971).

"Some kinds of pictures and geometric forms spontaneously shift in their principal aspect when they are looked at steadily. The reason probably lies in the physical organization of the perceptual system."

Gombrich, E. H., *"The Visual Image,"* (September, 1972).

"What a picture means to the viewer is strongly dependent on his past experience and knowledge. In this respect the visual image is not a mere representation of reality but a symbolic system."

Gregory, R. L., *"Visual Illusions,"* (November, 1968).

"Why do simple figures sometimes appear distorted or ambiguous? Perhaps because the visual system has to make sense of a world in which everyday objects are normally distorted by perspective."

Haber, R. N., *"How We Remember What We See,"* (May, 1970).

"It depends on whether what we see is pictorial (scenes, photographs and so forth) or linguistic (words, numbers and so on). Experiments indicate that the linguistic memory is different from the pictorial."

Hess, E. H., *"Attitude and Pupil Size,"* (April, 1965).

"Dilation and constriction of the pupils reflect not only *changes in light intensity, but also ongoing mental activity. The response is a measure of interest, emotion, thought processes and attitudes."*

Metelli, F., *"The Perception of Transparency,"* (April, 1974).

"Certain mosaics of opaque colors and shapes give rise to the impression of transparency. A simple theoretical model predicts the conditions under which perceptual transparency will occur."

Miller, G. A., *"Information and Memory,"* (August, 1956).

"If a man sees six marbles, he can usually name their numbers without counting. With more marbles, he often makes mistakes. This indicates a limitation of perception that is overcome by resourceful stratagems."

Neisser, V., *"Visual Search,"* (June, 1964).

"The cognitive operations involved in looking for a face in a crowd or a word in a list can be studied by timing the scanning process. Apparently many such operations can be carried out simultaneously."

Norton, D. and L. Stark, *"Eye Movements and Visual Perception,"* (June, 1971).

"Recordings of the points inspected in the scanning of a picture and of the path the eyes follow in the inspection provide clues to the process whereby the brain perceives and recognizes objects."

Ratliff, F., *"Contour and Contrast,"* (June, 1972).

"We see contours when adjacent areas contrast sharply. Surprisingly certain contours, in turn, make large areas appear lighter or darker than they really are. What neural mechanisms underlie these effects?"

Teuber, M. L., *"Sources of Ambiguity in the Prints of Maurits C. Escher,"* (July, 1974).

"The fascinating graphic inventions of the late Dutch artist reflect a strong mathematical and crystallographic influence. Their original inspiration, however, came from experiments on visual perception."

Addition

PAPERBACKS

Albers, J., *Interaction of Color.*
New Haven, CT: Yale Univ. Press, 1972.

A classic book on color based on Professor Albers' experiences at the Bauhaus and his teaching at Black Mountain College and Yale.

Behrens, R., *Art and Camouflage.*
Cedar Falls, Iowa: Univ. of Northern Iowa, 1981.

A unique book which traces and relates the history of camouflage to Gestalt psychology, Dadaism, Surrealism, Cubism and the Bauhaus.

Lanners, E., *Illusions.*
NY: Holt, Rinehart and Winston, 1977.

Almost everything you wanted to know and see about illusions and more. A fun book.

Zakia, R. and Todd, H., *Color Primer I and II*
Dobbs Ferry, NY: Morgan and Morgan, 1974.

An interactive programmed text that teaches both the additive (television) and subtractive (painting, printing, photography) systems of color mixtures. A set of six color filters is included.

Zakia, R., *Perceptual Quotes for Photographers.*
Rochester, NY: Light Impressions, 1980.

Over 500 selected quotations by 117 authors from a variety of disciplines: anthropology, art, literature, psychology, psychiatry, photography, science, theology.

HARDBACKS

Kepes, G., *Language of Vision.*
Chicago, IL: Paul Theobald and Company, 1969.

An early classic written in 1939. It deals with the problems of visual expression from a practical and humanistic perspective. The first chapter is an excellent presentation of Gestalt principles. Professor Kepes established and was the first Director of the Center of Advanced Visual Studies at MIT.

Stroebel, L., Todd, H., Zakia, R., *Visual Concepts for Photographers.*
Woburn, MA: Focal Press/Butterworth, 1980.

The authors have selected 150 visual concepts which relate directly to photography, illustration and design. Each concept consists of two pages; a word page which tells and a facing picture page which shows.

Weber, E., *Vision, Composition and Photography.*
Berlin/NY: Walter de Gruyter, 1980.

A highly visual and innovative book which relates design principles to photographic composition. The author is a professor of photography in Berlin.

Gardner, M., "Mathematical Games", (January, 1975).

"The curious magic of anamorphic art . . . it refers to realistic art so monstrously distorted by a projective transformation that it is difficult to recognize."

Gilchrist, A., "The Perception of Surface Blacks and Whites", (March, 1979).

"What shade of gray a surface appears is related to the perceived distribution of light and shadow, which in turn depends on the perceived spatial relation between the surface and its neighbors."

Gillam, B., "Geometrical Illusions", (January, 1980).

"In these classic figures of psychology lines appear different from the way they really are. The effects appear to be related to clues to the size of objects in the three-dimensional world."

Gogel, W., "The Adjacency Principle in Visual Perception", (May, 1978).

"The visual system integrates information about objects from different sources including relative, or contextual, cues. The adjacency principle describes how relative cues are weighted to achieve this integration."

Kanizsa, G., "Subjective Contour", (April, 1976).

"Certain combinations of incomplete figures give rise to clearly visible contours even when the contours do not actually exist. It appears that such contours are supplied by the visual system."

Siegel, R., "Hallucinations", (October, 1977).

"These false perceptions, which can occur in any of the senses, turn out to be much alike from one person to another. Apparently they have their roots in excitations of the central nervous system."

Walker, J., "The Amateur Scientist", (May, 1980).

"Illusions in the snow: more fun with random dots on the television screen."

Walker, J., "The Amateur Scientist", (July, 1981).

"Anamorphic pictures: distorted views from which distortion can be removed."

Yellott, J., "Binocular Depth Inversion", (July, 1981).

Sometimes a solid object seen with both eyes can seem to reverse perspective. A study of this geometrically irrational experience suggests that ordinary depth perception is somewhat precarious."

Index

All Stars 117
Amen 141
Area 43, 45, 46
Arnheim, Rudolph 82–83
Arrows 114
Artists:
  Blake, William 63
  Escher 24
  Voltz, Johann M. 16
  Wood, Grant 50, 51
Camouflage 76, 130
Canadian Capers 140
Candy Bars 113
Closed Areas 71
Closure 66, 87, 95, 143
Cloud Watching 128
Computer-Generated "Dots"
  123
Continuation and Closure 96
Continuation and Proximity 62
Continuity 59, 65, 87
Contour Line 72
Contrast 46
Cosmetologists 31
Cropping 135
Dalmatian Figure-Ground 151
Don't Be A Square 150, 154
Dot's Nice 121, 152
Editing 39, 65
Equivalents 128
Exponents 40
Factors 40
Figure-Ground 19, 20–31, 89,
  151
Find the Star 147
Flags 60, 66–67
Florists 31
Flower Arranging 134
Framing 39, 135
Ganzfeld 18
Geometric Form 74
Gestalt 15
Gestalt Exercises 112, 151
Gestalt Games 136
Gestalt Laws 32, 78, 85
Gestalt Psychology 15
Graininess 26
Graphic Designers:
  Bass, Saul 124
  Carapella, Harvey 108
  Chapman, Steve 24
  Coiner, Charles 124
  Geismar, Tom 58
  Montgomery, Bruce 124
  Morin, Tom 24
  Mutchnick, Sherman 136

Remington, Roger 141
Tyler, Latham 136
Graphic Summary 108
Graphic Symbols 21, 58, 109–111
Graphic Trademarks 43, 58, 124
Greasy Graphics 145
"Ground" Watching 129
Halftone Screen 46
Heterogeneous Field 18
Hide and Seek 146
Homogeneous Field 18
Information Theory 83
Isomorphism 128
Koffka, K. 20, 79
Law of Pragnanz 79, 81
Layout 62, 133
Light a Candle 120
Look Around 116
Mad, Fold-In 37
More Dots 122
Motion Pictures 65
Mounting 135
Music 39
Neutral Density Filters 40
Noise 26
Order and Complexity 82
Painting 50
Paper Clips 118
Percept 80, 81
Photographers:
  Agostino, Robert W. 53
  Atget, Eugene 71
  Atkin, Jonathan 106, 107
  Avedon, Richard 57
  Barr, Neal 104
  Bresson, Henri Cartier 69,
    91, 92, 96
  Brigman, A. 97
  Calder, Scott 49
  Davidhazy, Andrew 95
  Davidson, Bruce 55
  DeWolfe, George 101
  Dowdell, John J. 88, 102, 145
  Edgerton, Harold 68
  Emerson, P. H. 97
  Gibson, Ralph 44
  Hagner, Jerry 22
  Heinecken, Robert F. 17
  Jackson, William Henry 73,
    90, 98
  Jones, Liza 135
  Katzel, James 42
  Massey, John 103
  McKnight, Larry 122
  Muybridge, E. 65
  Myers, Barry 89
  Perlmutter, Abbey 101
  Remington, Roger 25
  Schottenfeld, R. 105
  Stieglitz, Alfred 128

Uelsmann, Jerry 36, 93
Weidert, George 116
Weston, Edward 60, 61
Wollwage, Mark 94, 128
Photographic Summary 88
Photo Rorschach 137
Positive-Negative Space 23
Pragnanz 79–81
Profiles 115
Proximity 32, 90
Proximity and Area 43
Proximity and Combination
  Printing 36
Proximity and Learning 40
Proximity and Similarity 92
Redundancy 83
Resolving Power 29
Resolving Power Targets 72
Rubin, Edgar 24
Same or Different 142
Save Stamps 125
Scrap Book 124
Screens (Projection) 28
Seeing and Saying 80
Sequences (and Continuity) 65
Signal to Noise Ratio 26
Similarity 47, 86, 91
Similarity and Closure 86
Similarity and Proximity 53
Similarity and Symmetry 57
Similarity of Meaning 54
Sketches (and Continuity) 63
Smell (and Figure-Ground) 30
Sound (and Figure-Ground) 30
Stops 40
Storyboarding 65
Summary (Graphic) 108
Summary (Photographic) 88
Summary (Verbal) 86
Symmetry 56, 93, 131
Symmetry and Graphic
  Symbols 58
Tactility (and Figure-Ground) 30
Tangrams 148, 153
Taste (and Figure-Ground) 30
Temporal Proximity 39
TV Screen 127
Typography 64, 119
Uncertainty 83
United Kingdom Flag 60
Verbal Figure-Ground 138
Verbal Summary 86
Video 65
Visual Elements 14, 86, 144
Visual-Tactile Puzzle (Answers)
  154
Wertheimer, Max 15, 79
What's in a Name? 23
Words 139
Words and Numbers 38